DUMITRU TSEPENEAG AND THE CANON OF ALTERNATIVE LITERATURE

Originally published in Romanian as *Dumitru Ţepeneag şi canonul literaturii alternative* by
Casa Cărţii de Ştiinţă, Cluj-Napoca, 2007

First edition, 2011

Library of Congress Cataloging-in-Publication Data

Pavel, Laura, 1968-
[Dumitru Tepeneag si canonul literaturii alternative. English]
Dumitru Tsepeneag and the canon of alternative literature / Laura Pavel ; translated by Alistair Ian Blyth. -- 1st ed.
p. cm.
Includes bibliographical references.
ISBN 978-1-56478-639-5 (pbk. : alk. paper)
1. Tepeneag, Dumitru, 1937---Criticism and interpretation. 2. Romanian literature--20th century--History and criticism. I. Title.
PC840.3.E67Z8313 2011
859'.334--dc22
2011012845

Partially funded by a grant from the Illinois Arts Council, a state agency, and by the University of Illinois at Urbana-Champaign

Partially funded by the Translation and Publication Support Program
of the Romanian Cultural Institute

www.dalkeyarchive.com

Cover: design and composition by Danielle Dutton

Printed on permanent/durable acid-free paper and bound in the United States of America

DUMITRU TSEPENEAG AND THE CANON OF ALTERNATIVE LITERATURE

BY LAURA PAVEL

TRANSLATED BY ALISTAIR IAN BLYTH

DALKEY ARCHIVE PRESS
CHAMPAIGN / DUBLIN / LONDON

CONTENTS

I.

ONEIRICISM—BETWEEN LITERARY HISTORY AND POLITICAL HISTORY

II.

FICTIONAL IDENTITY AND ONEIRIC IMAGOLOGY

III.

THE LONELINESS OF THE DEMIURGE CONFRONTED WITH THE EMANCIPATION OF THE CHARACTER

DUMITRU TSEPENEAG AND THE CANON OF ALTERNATIVE LITERATURE

I.

ONEIRICISM—BETWEEN LITERARY HISTORY AND POLITICAL HISTORY

The oneiricists and their aesthetic "proximities," inside and outside the literary/political canon of the 1970s • An aesthetic/extra-aesthetic, comparative, and historicist perspective • The aesthetic and subversive/political intentions of the oneiric group • Oneiric theory and its main promoter, Dumitru Tsepeneag • Writers and theorists: Dumitru Tsepeneag, Leonid Dimov, Daniel Turcea, Sorin Titel, Virgil Tănase, Vintilă Ivănceanu, Virgil Mazilescu, Emil Brumaru, Florin Gabrea, Iulian Neacşu[1]

The explanation for the emergence of the oneiric group in the Romania of the 1970s certainly resides in the more than abundant literary-theoretical vocation of Dumitru Tsepeneag, one of the most important prose writers of recent decades and the principal "ideologue" of Oneiricism. A contextual analysis of oneiric poetry and prose, as well as of the theory of *structural* or *aesthetic Oneiricism*, highlights a primarily aesthetic motivation and aim, but these are also, subsidiarily, political. A late-modernist

1 For references and further information about Romanian literary figures, see Glossary.

movement, with an aesthetic program which, as I shall argue, went against not only the Romanian but also the western literary and socio-political grain, Oneiricism also arose from the pressing need for a subversive gesture against official cultural policy and the pseudo-aesthetic direction of socialist realism. The motivations for the appearance of oneiric literature, as they are formulated in the critical discourse and theoretical manifestoes and prospectuses (in particular those by Tsepeneag and Dimov) that legitimize the movement, symptomatically blend aesthetic and political criteria. I think that what can be discovered here is a symptomatology of the crisis produced by the discrepancy between the historical moment, that of the post-Stalinist, post-socialist-realist communism of 1965–1968, and the literary moment.

In its nature, the subversiveness of Oneiricism is both implicit, relating to widespread formula of aesthetic subversion and shot through with Aesopian allusions to totalitarian abuses of power, and, sometimes, explicit, declared and analyzed as such by Dumitru Tsepeneag and in the West after 1971. The year in which Nicolae Ceauşescu formulated his "July Theses," which laid out a Maoist-style cultural revolution, 1971 marked a critical moment in Romanian politics and a crossroads for the Romanian intelligentsia. It was also the year that saw the disintegration of the oneiric group, its members harried by the ideological censorship of those times. The very term "oneiric" was outlawed. In the thought-provoking series of dialogues on aesthetic topics and on literary/political history that Romanian critic Ion Simuţ conducted with Tsepeneag a few years ago, the theoretician of Oneiricism, with the acuity of a historian of mentalities and political scientist, retrospectively characterized the transition period from socialist realism ("proletcultism") to the return of the aesthetic in the 1970s as follows: "There was a move away from *proletcultism* in the Gheorghiu-Dej period, and Ceauşescu inherited a certain liberalism in the arts, which he tried to get rid of in 1971. But that's not all. The Party realized at a given moment that art and literature were useless and dangerous servants, which could have all kinds of pretensions beyond their own field. And so it was that in the 1970s and '80s political censorship was tightened on the one hand, while there was a certain liberalism from the aesthetic point of view on the other: young writers could experiment as much as they liked, if that was what they wanted, as long as they didn't venture to make any political protest. After the downfall of the regime, this was what was called 'resistance through culture.' This aesthetic liberalism could be seen above all in translations from foreign literatures. I translated the nouveau roman. Later, there were even translations of 'bourgeois' theory (I think that even Jean Ricardou was translated, among others). The ignorance of the 1950s no longer existed." [2]

For example, the positioning of oneiric texts against the grain of the duplicitous literature that coexisted much more docilely with the censorship of the Ceauşescu regime—the so-called literature of the "obsessive decade"—seems to me to have the same importance, at the level of the aesthetic and cultural politics, as Oneiricism's polemical relationship with romanticism

2 Dumitru Ţepeneag, *Clepsidra răsturnată. Convorbiri cu Ion Simuţ, urmate de o "Addenda"* [*The Upended Sandglass. Conversations with Ion Simuţ, followed by an Addenda*] (Piteşti: Editura Paralela 45, 2003), 123–124.

and surrealism. Ultimately, the demystification[3] practiced by the literature of the "obsessive decade" (between 1950 and 1960), appearing after 1965, whose favorite theme was the drama of Communist Party members persecuted under Stalinism and their heroism when confronted with the abuses of the Gheorghiu-Dej period, "always has limits and is carried out only within certain conventions."[4] The relative nature of "the truth," a truth in any case truncated and ideologically airbrushed, as it was formulated by the prose of the obsessive decade, comes to light in any approach to it through the lens of the expectations of a wholly demystifying retrospective critical reading, that of the post-1989 period. The dose of duplicity to be found in the critical realist literature of the 1970s and '80s, which at the time was allusive and perhaps even subversive, today emerges more emphatically than its dose of courage, a courage that was not at all explicit and only vaguely dissident in relation to hard-line literary propaganda. Moreover, it is precisely the supposedly "courageous" subject matter of a part

---

3 Romanian essayist Sanda Cordoş captures the paradoxical ethic of literature under Ceauşescu, which fulfilled not only a civic function, that of a discourse of truth, thereby providing a counterpoint to the fiction of totalitarian ideology, but also a fictional function properly speaking, one constitutive of its nature, around which it redefined itself when accused of political disobedience: "The fact of (nevertheless) being a fiction that speaks the truth, opposing the (ideological) 'truth' that institutes fictions, ensured a protective ambiguity for literature: when it corners a mystified reality, attempting to unravel it, the attack occurs in the name of the Truth, but when the Mystifier (power) prepares to suppress its audacity, literature will draw back, defending itself behind the shield of fiction." *Literatura între revoluţie şi reacţiune. Problema crizei în literatura română şi rusă a secolului XX* [*Literature between Revolution and Reaction: The Problem of the Crisis in Twentieth-Century Romanian and Russian Literature*] (Cluj: Editura "Biblioteca Apostrof," 1999), 169.

4 Ibid., 170.

of pre-1989 literature, valued as incendiary at the time, that in the post-December-Revolution period becomes "dated," susceptible to duplicitous hypocrisy and unavoidable aesthetic and ideological half-truths, viciously combining both.

In the case of the oneiric group, on the other hand, the situation seems to be exactly the reverse: an apparently non-topical (or "untimely," to use Nietzsche's term, but without the philosopher's polemic against the modern culture of progress) problematic, albeit one that can be integrated into late modernism, becomes not only *timely* today, decades later, but also *forward-looking* in relation to the aesthetic taste of the near future. What are the arguments for the timeliness of this literature? Do they primarily bear upon, let us say, the neo-avant-garde form of oneiric innovation, as a method of textual creation and structuring? Are they connected with the self-referential meaning of this already textualist literature, prior to the "textualism" of the Eighties Generation in Romanian literature? Or can such arguments be found in the non-ideological content of the oneiric problematic, which wagers upon a future audience, precisely due to its rejection of subjects affected by politics, or rather by the themes of socialist realism and the obsessive decade, to be more precise? Is Oneiricism not only a provocative textualizing strategy, justifiable as a coherent poetic and literary-typological choice, but also a literary movement with political implications? If I succeed in arguing that things stand thus, then this moment in literary-political history might seem an aporia of the ghostly "autonomy of the aesthetic" in the post-Stalinist period of the 1960s, when the first theorizations of structural Oneiricism emerge. For how can the paradox of the sometimes voluntary, sometimes unavoidable, politicization of a declaredly aesthetic means of creation, one even accused of evasiveness during times of censorship, appear otherwise than surprising?

More than once, Romanian literature of the 1960s accomplished a self-preserving resumption of the history that had been brutally interrupted by Stalinist ideology and socialist realism. Hence results a recuperation of its aesthetic substance by means of a "regressive evolutionary motion."[5] Oneiricism, by contrast, is, par excellence, progressive and forward-looking, and when it seeks its roots in the Romanian literary past or in the mature modernism of the likes of Ion Barbu, it wishes only to *invent* its own tradition. The proclamation of canonic models is made in order to attenuate

5 In connection with the need to rewrite and rethink the canon of Romanian modernity, Ion Bogdan Lefter (a well-known Romanian critic of the Eighties Generation) formulates a provocative polemical thesis regarding the art of the decades following proletcultism, dominated by neo-modernism. According to Lefter, the regressive neo-type evolution was due to a deviated cultural metabolism and to a desire to compensate for the cultural hiatus of the 1950s: "Scorning the anachronism of the rhetoric of power in the 1950s, the representative artists of the decade that followed were condemned by circumstances to a different anachronism, this time imposed not by the artificial propaganda of the political regime, but by the so-to-speak 'natural' metabolism of national cultural history, which obliged them to take part in the healing of the proletcultist sickness by repairing the tissues where they were torn. The 'new' formulas they explored with enthusiasm represent a step forward compared with the neo-folklore and neo-naturalist discourses of socialist realism, but do nothing more than reconstitute the range of rhetorics in fashion during the first half of the twentieth century." The critic also recognizes, however, the existence of a minority experimentalism, which anticipates Romanian postmodernism. Oneiricism and the convergence between the nouveau roman and the prose of Tsepeneag would belong to authentic experiment. See Ion Bogdan Lefter, *Postmodernism. Din dosarul unei "bătălii" culturale* [*Postmodernism. From the Dossier of a Cultural "Battle"*] (Piteşti: Editura Paralela 45, 2000), 100–101.

something of the movement's exuberant avant-garde projection of itself. The oneiricists retroactively supply even their own tradition, in order to promote themselves before an audience that desires to experience not only the frisson of innovation but also the pleasure of *recognizing* already established literary reference points. Or else in order to establish and confirm theoretically the organic character of a new textual poetics, while also reconfirming the eternal aporia of modernity/tradition.

*

While Leonid Dimov, the "witch doctor of the oneiric tribe," was the group's most important poet and, at times, essayist, Dumitru Tsepeneag was simultaneously the prose writer and comparative theorist who persevered in explicating not only the Romanian roots of the method and structure of oneiric literature, but also its aspirations to synchronicity and the symptoms of its phasing with the literary and European cultural context. In an article published in *Gazeta literară* [*The Literary Gazette*] in 1968, entitled "Vase comunicante" ["Communicating Vessels"], Tsepeneag deplores the anachronistic condition of Romanian prose in relation to poetry, as well as the incapacity of contemporary criticism when confronted with prose that defies the traditional canons. Advocating, by means of aesthetic, anthropological and cultural political arguments, the natural synchronization of Romanian literature with modern literature more generally, the theorist of the oneiric method observes: "Let us not forget that, although before the War we had almost succeeded in integrating ourselves into the context of European literature, afterwards there followed a period of regress, of a weakened sense of belonging to the modern, European spirit. We are now trying to make up lost ground. (. . .) Why should we not accept the idea of communicating vessels, a theory so beautifully argued by the Romanian critic Eugen Lovinescu? It is highly natural that people of the same epoch should think similarly and should express themselves in similar ways."[6] Invoking the innovative calling of a number of Romanian artists and writers, Tsepeneag is probably thinking of avant-gardists such as Tristan Tzara and Constantin Brâncuşi, who left Romania to become the founders of movements or at least artistic styles at the European level. The theorist and prose writer is here polemicizing against the conservative critics who invalidly accused native Romanian literary experimenters of being epigones and imitators. He urges Romanian authors to activate their lucid tendency toward synchronization with Europe: "Why is it that we explain the newer trends in our literature as an imitative phenomenon? There have been so many artists who have set out from these lands and then affirmed themselves as innovative figures. Now that we have entered into a normal rhythm of development, it is absolutely necessary that our literature should be in conscious synchronization with the evolution of modern, universal literature."[7] But on the one hand, Tristan Tzara, Constantin Brâncuşi, and Eugène Ionesco (and

6 Dumitru Ţepeneag, "Vase comunicante," in *Gazeta literară*, no. 31, August 1, 1968, 7; see also Leonid Dimov, Dumitru Ţepeneag, *Momentul oniric* [*The Oneiric Moment*], ed. Corin Braga (Bucharest: Editura Cartea Românească, 1997), 46.

7 Ibid., 47.

also Urmuz, although less known in the West) are structurally European authors, not exactly symptomatic of Romanian culture as a whole, which has a substantial dose of conservative traditionalism. On the other hand, this culture, barely having emerged from somber Stalinist socialist realism, was to enter into a long-desired phase of "normality" only in appearance and only for a short period.

A judgment that is lucid precisely because it is retrospective, freed from any illusions regarding a transient cultural-political "springtime," was also formulated by Tsepeneag in Paris, in 1974, within a theoretical and literary-historical article about the context in which Oneiricism had arisen, published firstly in *Les Lettres Nouvelles* and later translated into Romanian by the author. In this landmark text, entitled "Tentativa onirică, după război" ["The Oneiric Endeavor, after the War"], Dumitru Tsepeneag remarks upon the increasingly accentuated intolerance of the Romanian cultural milieu in the period leading up to the outbreak of the Second World War. The Romanian avant-garde was persecuted not only by fascism and the right-wing parties but also by Stalinism, which persisted in Romania longer than elsewhere. Immediately after the War, in the short period before the imposition of Stalinism, the Romanian surrealists reached creative boiling point, also displaying some left-wing "revolutionary" political accents. Whereas before the War, during the period when he contributed to *unu* [*one*] magazine, Geo Bogza had placed an emphasis upon the subversive nature of dreams, after the War Gherasim Luca propounded the "total dream," purified of "diurnal reactionary residues," as well as the perpetuation of a social-revolutionary atmosphere through the "limitless eroticization of the proletariat." The marginal geographic and cultural position they held in relation to their western counterparts caused the Romanian surrealists to formulate aesthetically and ideologically "extremist" positions. Gherasim Luca and Trost, for example, proved more orthodox than their pre-War antecedents and allowed themselves to be led by "a frenzy I might venture to call provincial," adds Tsepeneag. Here, however, provincialism does not have a pejorative nuance, but rather it is a label whereby the theorist denounces the limits of the surrealists' ideological manifestations around the year 1945, while accepting them with a disillusioned but sympathetic backward look at the recent past. His analysis of past sociology and mindsets, which places the post-War Romanian avant-garde in the difficult social and political context of the 1940s, even before the Stalinist period, does not lack a skeptical note, but also displays a certain retrospective solidarity with the often eccentric enthusiasms of the avant-garde fraternity under the influence of "their times": "After May 1968, and in the circumstances well described by Marcuse, all these ideas appear to us today as less absurd, although still utopian. In any case, Deleuze would subscribe to them.[8] The manifesto "Dialectica dialecticii" ["The Dialectic of the Dialectic"] by Gherasim Luca and D. Trost (the latter being the author of the theory of *superautomatism*) is imbued with "revolutionary" ideas dramatic in their ridiculousness. For Luca,

8 See the comments by Dumitru Tsepeneag on the surrealism of the period immediately after the war in "Tentativa onirică, după război," in *Momentul oniric*, 212–213.

for example, the Oedipus complex is deleterious to the struggle of the working class, as long as the "class enemy," identical with "the father," lurks in the blood of the proletariat.

Another socio-politically engaged surrealist group included the matchless Gellu Naum (whose "Depoetizați universul" ["Depoeticize the Universe"] paradoxically leads to its re-mythicizing, with only traditional poetics being rejected), Paul Păun and Virgil Teodorescu, self-proclaimed Marxists and at the same time Hegelians. They propose a revolutionary intensification of everyday life, not only of art, and in this period accuse Luca and Trost of reactionary conformism. After 1960, when the surrealists make their timid reappearance on the cultural stage, "censorship of the consciousness disappears, but Party censorship remains. Whether automatic or not, writing is in any case dictated by the Party."[9] The old surrealists no longer have any impact, and only Gellu Naum is revalorized, although he does not make any real comeback until after 1989, inclusively as a playwright. But during the short cultural "thaw," a number of talented young writers of a certain surrealist lineage do manage to make a name for themselves.

The oneiric group was one such constellation of authors, even if it was to define its method and literary typology through a polemical relationship to surrealism, rejecting the latter's psychoanalytical scientism and the doctrine of automatic writing. Its history, as it is narrated by the group's protagonist and "chronicler," Dumitru Tsepeneag, includes a period of clandestinity ("no one wanted to publish us"), that of the friendship with Leonid Dimov, when its

9 Ibid., 215.

theoretic gestation took place, between 1959 and 1964. In 1965, at the *Luceafărul* [*The Lucifer*] magazine literary cenacle, Tsepeneag met Virgil Mazilescu, Vintilă Ivănceanu, and Iulian Neacşu, who were to make up the oneiric group. In 1966, the oneiricists published their work in the literary supplement of *Ramuri* [*Branches*] review, entitled *Povestea vorbii* [*The Story of the Saying*], edited by Miron Radu Paraschivescu in Craiova, in which they were naturally censored, while the small publication was banned only a few months later. After an abortive attempt to publish a group magazine, in 1968 Dumitru Tsepeneag published in four successive issues of *Luceafărul* magazine a series of programmatic articles entitled "În căutarea unei definiţii" ["In Search of a Definition"].[10] A few months later, in the student magazine *Amfiteatru*, a round-table discussion entitled "O modalitate artistică" ["An Artistic Modality"] was published, basically a kind of manifesto, signed by Leonid Dimov, Daniel Turcea, Laurenţiu Ulici, and, of course, Tsepeneag.

In spite of having been censored, the manifesto still managed to arouse the ire of the authorities, which did not tolerate any solidarity other than the ideological solidarity artificially fostered by the propagandists of the single party. "The persecution that follows," Tsepeneag specifies, "must also be placed in connection with the invasion of Czechoslovakia by Soviet troops. They were tightening the screw, so that others would not come to tighten it for them. But this persecution above all relates to the oneiric theory; for better or worse, our writing still managed to appear in print. Other writers also adopted the 'oneiric model,' thereby

10 *Luceafărul*, no. 25, 22 June 1968, 7; no. 26, 29 June 1968, 7; no. 27, 6 July 1968, 6; no. 28, 13 July 1968, 6.

discovering a means of escape from the dilemma with which the countries of the Eastern bloc were struggling: either to tell the truth and risk being censored and negatively targeted, or to write in a socialist-realist manner, i.e. a varnished, conformist literature."[11] Other talented writers joined the group, such as Sorin Titel and Virgil Tănase. Some gave up any oneiric affiliation, such as Iulian Neacşu. And others still left the country, such as Vintilă Ivănceanu. In the end, the group gradually lost its unity, while the coup de grâce was dealt by Ceauşescu's July Theses in 1971.

11 Ibid., 216.

THE PRINCIPAL THESES OF AESTHETIC ONEIRICISM

The relationship of Oneiricism to various aesthetics of the dream • Oneiricism versus lyricism: a relationship of "mutual suspicion" (Dumitru Tsepeneag) • The objectivism and non-metaphorical nature of Dimov's lyric poetry versus the abstraction and metaphysical lyric metaphors of Nichita Stănescu • The oneiric method as a "play of forces" (Leonid Dimov) • The "wave-particle" (Daniel Turcea), a property of the word in oneiric writing

Oneiric poetry and prose more often than not seem dislocated from any social or political "reality," a reality that was often hallucinatory, ideologically fictionalized through distorting and schizoid utopian edicts. The oneiric discourses in poetry and in prose are structured as *texts* increasingly conscious of their own textuality, a textuality that is autonomous in relation to the potential referent and creates seemingly aseptic and autarchic fictional worlds. In his series of theoretical articles "In Search of a Definition," Dumitru Tsepeneag puts forward a ludic, theatrical characterization of the romantic *dream*, from which Oneiricism partly separates itself, although it recognizes and perpetuates a number of its eternal cultural invariables:

> [The romantics] looked, if I can put it this way, *into dream*, the same as you look through a keyhole. For, what is the dream if not that strange spectacle of voyeurism, scenes seen through the keyhole, and the simultaneous fear and joy of being alone, omniscient and ubiquitous, in an objective world, where people, too, become objects, where there is no relationship, where there is no social or political velleity. There is probably no God there, although it is as if He were.[12]

It is possible to analyze here the *theatrical gaze* of the creator of textual *dreams*, a gaze that successively empathizes with and then distances itself from what is seen. This "it is as if He were" is the creative mimesis of romantic oneiric literature, which has quasi-mystical reverberations and causes the presence of transcendence to be verisimilar. And the world of "as if" triggers a certain type of catharsis, thanks to the fascination of clandestine contemplation, a theatrical "voyeurism" that is also characteristic of Tsepeneag as a prose writer. Moreover, he even entitles one of his parabolic prose pieces, one that is fundamental with regard to the cosmogonic motions of the text and of oneiric imagery, precisely "Prin gaura cheii" ["Through the Keyhole"].

---

12 See the distinctions Ţepeneag makes between romanticism, surrealism and oneiricism in "În căutarea unei definiţii," in *Momentul oniric*, 25.

Whereas the dreams of ancient literature were premonitory or prophetic, conveying to men a message from the gods, in the Middle Ages they were to become primarily moral, rather than supernatural, combining Christian symbolic images and inscribing them as a palimpsest over pre-existing myths. There follows a period in which the dream becomes conventional, an "object of psychological and, more rarely, philosophical curiosity." Thanks to the separation of the sacred from the profane, in the Renaissance and thereafter, European classicism arrives at a "crisis of the imagination," in which images of heaven and hell, occurring more and more rarely, sooner become conventionalized ideas. Gradually, Christian miracles and at the same time "the mythology artificially revived by the Renaissance and beloved of classicism" give way to a "purely artistic supernatural," a process consummated by romanticism and then by means of the aesthetic "gratuitousness" of modern art.[13] In the provisory system of categories into which Tsepeneag separates the "aesthetics of the dream," the Oneiricism of the 1970s is distinct from the procedure of invoking the dream, which, from the ancients onward, was lacking in aesthetic autonomy, as well as from the "fantasy of ignorance," to be found in the Middle Ages, and the medieval moralizing and didactic oneiric.

Aesthetic Oneiricism is no less defined by means of a theoretical dynamism, which constructs, through polemic but also an often nostalgic reverence for the past, an entire aesthetic of the *fertile contrast*. This is a contrast with the "philosophical or metaphysical" oneiric of the romantics, as well as with the

13 Ibid., 26–27.

"psychoanalytical" or "scientific" oneiric of the surrealists. In this way there arises the theoretic innovation on which oneiric literature is nourished and, conversely, meta-textual literature often itself becomes a fictionalized subject, within a continuous circle of self-generating textuality: "Finally, the oneiric which I shall baptize simply *aesthetic*, a category in which the dream is no longer an artistic means of moralization, or a source of metaphysical revelations, or a 'scientific' method of venting frustrations through art; rather it is quite simply a criterion, a limit term for comparison or, as Leonid Dimov would say, a *suggestion for the legislation* of an independent art, but one that is analogous to reality."[14]

In the final part of his theoretical "feuilleton," Tsepeneag confesses his disappointment at the fact that his comparative distinctions and references for the circumscription of Oneiricism have provoked false, unfounded polemics, because these are not based on a careful reading of his arguments. These opportunist critics, be they of different aesthetic allegiances, be they those who castigated Oneiricism with the blessing of the Party and its propaganda apparatus,[15] seemed not to understand the essential difference between dream as a *source* of inspiration and dream as defined by the oneiricists as a *criterion*, a term of comparison. The sole authentic objection would be that according to which, subsequent to Tsepeneag's demonstration, it might seem that any

14 Ibid., 30.

15 For some tendentious critics, oneiricism is apparently a "literature of falling asleep" (Marian Popa, "Proza lui D. Țepeneag" [The Prose of . . .], in *Luceafărul*, no. 9, 2 March 1968, 2), and the prose-writer is supposed to cultivate a kind of "parable without any didactic meaning, too hermetic in its vocabulary to have any inner meaning" (Al. Piru, "Literatura absurdului" [The Literature of the Absurd], in *Luceafărul*, no. 12, 23 March 1968, 3).

poetry is absorbed by or tends to be included in the seemingly over-inclusive sphere of the oneiric.

*

At this point, Tsepeneag's polemical arguments draw upon an analysis of genres and species that might almost be called pedantic. A number of nuances of the traditional poetry/prose dichotomy are lovingly placed under the aesthetic microscope, with the aim of advancing, based upon them, new analytical distinctions and theoretic hypotheses.

The old classification according to *lyrical* or *epic* seems more legitimate to Tsepeneag, given that the criteria for separating prose works from poetic texts have become unstable, have been thrown into doubt. For example, the *ambiguity* specific to literature, i.e. the semantic diffusion from context and subtext, is also to be found in prose—the parables of Kafka being regarded as exemplary in this sense—not only in poetry, and even less so only in poetry that is lyrical in the proper sense. Moreover, Tsepeneag puts forward a surprising hypothesis, but one which, through subsequent stringent demonstration, he makes aesthetically plausible: "I might say even the contrary, adding that the oneiric and the lyrical find themselves in a relationship of mutual mistrust."[16] There follows a provocative comparison between the lyrical poetry of Nichita Stănescu (for whom the metaphor is necessary, because it "concentrates reality, it 'swallows' time and accelerates the speed of the poetic line"), a poetry with highly abstract accents, and the

16 *Momentul oniric*, 31.

oneiric poetry of Leonid Dimov, a poetry that is sooner epic, to a certain extent objective, and lacking in metaphors: "I wish merely to underline the tendency of Nichita Stănescu, a lyrical poet par excellence (albeit one who is sometimes pseudo-philosophical), toward an increasingly abstract poetry, not so much in his terms as much as in the effects that result from the clash between them. Here there is a splendid adventure of speed, as if in a dream in the middle of the night, which gives you the impression of lasting an eternity but which in reality lasts two or three minutes or even less. A dream that cannot, however, be narrated, but in the best case merely suggested by means of a felicitous metaphor . . . Reading Dimov, what leaps to the eye from the very start is the lack of metaphors. Dimov describes, enumerates, inventories, and this is why he requires ever more space; his poetic line has a lazy, slowed-down movement (that of the epic); his exclamations are made up of verbs in the imperative; in fact he tells a story, he narrates a vision analogous to that in a dream, but one that is *made*, is rationally constructed; in the end, I wonder whether the latest poems and 'dreams' of Dimov can still be called poems. I would call them oneiric texts pure and simple."[17]

In Tsepeneag's view, Leonid Dimov is thus more an author of "texts" than of lyric poems, which, I think, also likens him to various poets of the Eighties Generation, in whom can be detected textualist reflections, but compensated by a sophisticated imagery with epic nuclei, such as Mariana Marin, Matei Vişniec and Ion Mureşan. The rejection of metaphor and lyrical abstraction and, alternatively, the recourse to an increasingly accentuated epic

17 Ibid., 32–33.

mode of poetry also liken Dimov to a few atypical poets of the 1990s, such as Daniel Bănulescu and Ioan Es. Pop. But Dimov belongs primarily to Oneiricism thanks to the acute visuality of his imagery, as well as his method—one that is expressionist in origin—of hyperbolically projecting a sentiment, thereby transforming it into an *object* that can be *viewed* by a seemingly trans-subjective eye. According to Tsepeneag, the paradoxical epic, non-lyrical poetry of the oneiricists presupposes a de-subjectivization of the one whose vocation is to view and to be viewed from without, in his objectivity and ubiquity, and to construct the dream-poem: "In dream, everything is seen, sometimes even thought. And the sensation of ubiquity ultimately leads to the complete disappearance of the 'I.' You no longer exist, you are nothing more than an eye."[18] The integration without remainder of oneiric texts into any of the traditional literary genres is inconceivable, claims Tsepeneag. The oneiric, concludes the group's theoretician, "seen categorically (thus in an ideal way), is in opposition to the lyrical and the metaphorical, but also to the epic, based on the law of causality."[19] Within the framework of the round table discussion published in *Amfiteatru* magazine in December 1968, Tsepeneag brings up a number of extremely pertinent distinctions with regard to the internal, non-Aristotelian logic of Oneiricism. Instead of formal, Aristotelian logic, the logic of cause and effect, oneiric literature resorts, out of a "purely aesthetic need,"[20] to non-causal

18 Ibid., 33.

19 Ibid., 34.

20 "O modalitate artistică" [An Artistic Modality]. Roundtable discussion with: Leonid Dimov, Dumitru Ţepeneag, Daniel Turcea, Laurenţiu Ulici, in *Momentul oniric*, 73. Following publication of the issue that contained this

sequence. The simultaneity specific to surrealist painting, but not to the automatic writing promoted by André Breton in literature, and rational control of infinite oneiric space-time are all specific to Oneiricism both in poetry and in prose.

In his turn, Leonid Dimov talks about the oneiric method in poetry, formulating extremely nuanced analyses of the way in which this "technique" might materialize: "The syntax acquires a kind of synesthetic illumination (and herein resides one of the essential distinctions between oneiric literature and Dadaism etc., movements for which syntax no longer represents an idol, but rather, sometimes, an enemy); the orthography—literally and figuratively—plays an obvious, almost calligrammatic, role, intended to chisel the rough edges of a multi-dimensioned language."[21] The words of oneiric literature would themselves become "*real* and *integral* elements," because the writer is no longer interested in resorting to their quality as symbols or notions. In addition, the orthographic signs, the form, position and size of the letters would have the seemingly *material* weight of "plastic elements." Their materiality is nevertheless relativized in Dimov's vision, and they are elements that ultimately possess a paradoxical, ghostly, somewhat holographic plasticity for him. Calligrammes, even as a prosodic frame, occur as so many ectoplasms, which sometimes congeal into solidity, like the Zburător [Flying Man] of Romanian folklore, erotically wed to the imaginary projections

---

roundtable discussion, the director of *Amfiteatru* magazine was fired. A memorandum of protest was collectively signed against this abusive decision.

21 Leonid Dimov, "În odaia Minotaurului. Încercare asupra artei onirice" [In the Chamber of the Minotaur: Essay on Oneiric Art], in *Momentul oniric*, 257–258.

of oneiric space-time: “The prosodic crust (I refer not only to poetry, but also to prose) prefigures—like the morphogenetic plan of arthropods—a *skeleton*, upon which will intervene the insertions of the visible organs (. . .) The countless procedures utilized in ‘ordinary’ literature become ‘literary acts in themselves’ and, the thing that is essential, to them all is added a coefficient without dimensions, but one that is profoundly extensible, which transforms the normal and normalizing element used in literature into a kind of play of forces that enters into a relationship with other plays of forces, forming entire groups of an ergic nature, i.e. capable of giving the reader the sensation of an intrinsic reality.”[22]

This idea, according to which the fictional-oneiric universe is a possessor of intrinsic meaning, without very clear relations with the exterior world, is also formulated by Daniel Turcea. To a certain extent convergent with what Dimov says about words’ “play of forces” and about their energy becoming corporealized in phantasms, Turcea defines an additional property of the same words constructed by the oneiric energy flux, named the *wave-particle*: “And then, taking the dream as a self-evident necessity, unrelated to that which is outside it, the words that encrypt this state acquire an additional property—that property which in modern physics is called the *wave-particle*—they become relative and by means of their relativity the fragment is contaminated by totality. The word thereby becomes the exponent of a series of qualitative fluxes that compresses the sensible and the ideal. The empty spaces between words, the *waves*, the suspension of speech, become so important that they construct words. And in this way

22 Ibid., 258.

to the word is restored its elementariness and origin. It is removed from its mold and can once again evolve without rigidity, atonally, polyphonically, monodically, incantatorily."[23] The oneirics will otherwise oscillate, in poetry and in prose, but also in the theory coeval with their work, between an emphasis upon the *autonomy of the text*, itself both object and referent, and the *trangressivity of the text*, which is inscribed and constructed as a meaningful but also discursive *event*, functioning as a bridge toward other artistic languages—musical, pictorial, theatrical, and cinematic.

Oneiric prose will also claim for itself a musical/polyphonic character, whose main proponent is Dumitru Tsepeneag, who not only argues in favor of the musical structure of textuality in his theoretical articles, but also achieves it in many of his short stories and novels. And the plays of force and the energy of the waves, in which, in the opinion of both Dimov and Turcea, oneiric discursivity, whether epic, lyrical or sooner hybrid, lyric-epic, was to be absorbed, seem to confer upon the text the weightlessness of a dream. What is imported from the dream into Oneiricism, as a literature of "complete lucidity" (Tsepeneag), is a new *legislation*, one that will form the object of numerous commentaries by Dimov and Tsepeneag. The new legislative criterion is invoked with the aim of re-ordering the elements of the real world.

23 Daniel Turcea, in "O modalitate artistică . . . ," in *Momentul oniric*, 73–74.

ONEIRIC ART AND THE OPENING OF THE CANON

The oneiric as a mode of invading reality • The new canon and tolerance of oneiric art, which "includes in the capacity of object of art both the center and the circumference" (Leonid Dimov) • Oneiric fiction, the rejection of the perverse fiction of totalitarian ideology, and socialist realism • Author/character/reader—a power relation? • Oneiricism / romanticism / surrealism / the absurd / the nouveau roman / textualism • Open canon and alternative literature

What connection can be made between the intrinsic aesthetic space, structured in accordance with an oneiric legislation, and the public space, all but fictionalized by means of ideological utopias and accepted hypocrisies in relationships between persons and towards authority? And what is the connection between the space-time specific to oneiric art and that of the socialist-realist literature contemporary with the oneiricists? What were the strategies of the oneiricists whereby they defined themselves in contrast to the dogmas of the other, servile literature, which accepted the compromise of self-ideologization in order to be tolerated and viewed more benignly by the censors and cultural propaganda of the time?

A number of paradoxical oneiric manifestations and poetics contain, and barely conceal, a continual conflictual tension in relation to the presupposed eye of the reader, be it that of the complicit, subversive reader, be it that of the censor. As early as the article entitled "Preambul" ["Preamble"], published in 1968, Leonid Dimov seems to adopt a dual strategy, a *defense by means of attack*, towards the accusation of escapism leveled at the oneiricists, as well as toward the suspicion of eventual detractors, adepts of a supposed "realism," one that was rigid and ultimately encysted in ideology. "The oneiric, as I understand it," declares Dimov, "is not a mode of escaping from reality, but on the contrary, one of invading it, of piercing as far as its skeleton, where the sensible world is replaced by its anterior hypostasis, by a *force*."[24] Given that it is not in the least intolerant or exclusive, oneiric literature also situates itself, in Dimov's apologia, within an ethical and aesthetic perspective of tolerance toward the marginal. This is what makes it, unintentionally and, I might add, surprisingly synchronic with the socio-cultural position of western postmodernists, especially those in America. The fissure between high and low culture seems to have been transcended, at least in intent, by the oneiricists: "The world of objects that oneiric art presupposes eliminates the antagonistic boundaries between

24 Leonid Dimov, "Preambul," in *Luceafărul*, no. 27, 6 July 1968, 7; see also *Momentul oniric*, 36.

phenomena, it transmutes values, i.e. it includes in the quality of *object* of art both the center and the circumference, both the backyard with dahlias and the terraces of great Second-Empire palaces, it views with an equal gaze both socialist-realist murals and fairy stories."[25] It is also Dimov, in the effort to make oneiric literature acceptable and to rid it of the accusation of solipsism and non-committed art, of art for art's sake, who advances an important cultural-ideological distinction: "It [oneiric literature] creates a new legislation in which the above-mentioned elements create a new world, one that is always more meaningful (literarily speaking), more alive, more powerful than the real world, one that provides *not the illusion of a certainty, but the certainty of an illusion*."[26] However, the formula *the certainty of an illusion* is, I think, aimed at the grave utopian and totalitarian self-delusion of an entire community, including its literary faction. And to bring this into "debate" through a polemical text is a strategy for *opening the reader's eyes*, in total critical lucidity, without any lapse into irresponsible blindness within dreaming or the sleep of reason.

Dimov deftly deflects the accusation of art for art's sake that the detractors of Oneiricism had formulated and in his turn directs it against the very art most opposed to the oneiric modernist aesthetic, namely against "dogmatic realism." Dogma embodied in the sphere of the aesthetic was another form of collective hypnosis, one more perverse, I might add, than propaganda properly speaking. Compared with jingoistic propaganda literature, what Dimov condescendingly calls dogmatic realism possessed in

25 Leonid Dimov, "Pledoarie pentru o artă optimistă – discuții" [Appeal for an Optimistic Art], in *Momentul oniric*, 39.

26 Leonid Dimov, "În odaia Minotaurului. Încercare asupra artei onirice," 259.

addition the argument of being art, as well as the accreditation conferred on it by the quantum of the ineffable provided by the authors' talent (often counterfeited with permission from the communist authorities). On the other hand, the ethical relevance of the oneiric program resides in the fact that it provides with lucidity, in those times contaminated and even hypnotized by totalitarian ideology, a sorely needed compensatory paradox: *the certainty of an illusion.* The certainty that we are spectators of a theatrical illusion causes the disappearance of "the photographic revelation of details, description for the sake of description, the psychological load artificially grafted onto insignificant gestures, in a word the countless formal or formalist elements that relate to the domain of art for art's sake, of aimless art, to put it maliciously, and to which, in spite of its opposition, dogmatic realism was never alien."[27] In his incarnation as inventive essayist, Dimov here makes a skillful attempt, albeit one ultimately doomed to failure, to push the boundaries of the ideological censors' tolerance. The writer, subject to the times, hoped that the censor's eye would allow Oneiricism a door, however narrow or out of the way, by which to enter the sphere of the literature accepted in the polis of the totalitarian utopia. Once inside the walls, the aim of Oneiricism was to act as a Trojan horse . . .

*

The strategy of penetrating the polis in which culture was controlled, in traumatic fashion, by politics also marks a number of the aesthetic positions of the oneiric program. Conversely, it

27 Ibid.

might be said that some of the declarations of intent and methods of oneiric writing paradoxically prove to be in agreement with the expositional perspective and bracingly optimistic tone the Party expected from artists. Of course, not only the subversive potential but also the anti-dogmatism supported by oneiric literature, a literature that was above all "politically suspect" (Thomas Mann's character Settembrini judged music in the same way), might make such a statement seem surprising. Did the oneiricists make little compromises with the guiding perspective of the propagandists who oriented the ideological line in culture? Categorically not, but what is remarkable is the speculative ability whereby Leonid Dimov, for example, comes to gloss over the apparently intrinsic optimism of oneiric art, the dream understood not as an unreality, but as a "component of global existence." Likewise, the way he glosses over the aggressive position of the oneiric aesthetic in relation to the audience's reality, which it invades and to which it responds through the representativeness of the legislation of the dream, which is an eternally human legislation.

In his dazzling remarks on the aesthetic program in the "Preamble," Dimov recognizes the *actively* poetic character of the oneiric lyric. The dynamism of the lyric is compared to lucidity, and the author emphasizes, in the more wide-ranging essay "În odaia Minotaurului" ["In the Chamber of the Minotaur"], the idea that the oneiric literary image is the result of a lucid creative combustion, and not of any surrealist-type trance: "Indeed, *a determined consistency* is the essential characteristic of the oneiric image. Arising from an ad hoc chaos, it is captured in the very moment of its coagulation and unleashed into the future oneiric 'world' as a variable potency. The variation and trajectory of this potency are determined by the creator in accordance with a legislation drawn up in the fraction of a second that precedes the act of creation. But not a fraction of a second of inspiration, of trance, of automatism, but of maximum lucidity, a kind of all-encompassing aura justified and absolved by the very process of its being made explicit in the work."[28]

Like a painting, an oneiric text is not the calculus or film sequence of a dream calqued from memory—since, as Dimov adds, with renewed polemical vigor, "we would then find ourselves confronted with an *à rebours* naturalism"—but rather it comes to investigate the real image with "that reactive power specific to the dream."[29] What is at stake in the construction of the oneiric image as a *variable potency* is the *actual* induction of a privileged dream state in the reader, a state that becomes more than merely a drug for author and reader alike: "Through the secret connection that is established between creator and reader, oneiric literature erases at a given point any distinction between them, conferring upon art an expositional role."[30] In this performance-type interaction between creator and reader, there is something of the future inter-creative collaboration of the virtual reality traveler, the recipient of virtual artistic creation, who himself becomes a demiurge of space-time conceived in its initial form by another, temporary and likewise virtual demiurge. The expositional and not at all elitist role of Oneiricism would therefore consist in the opportunity

28 Ibid., 260.

29 Ibid.

30 Ibid.

the reader is offered to conceive of himself as a creator in his turn. An active creator-spectator, who, through the intermediate formula of complicity with the writer and of projection into the latter's position as demiurge, transposes his own experiences and phantasms onto the text, lucidly ordering them in accordance with the paralogical legislation of the dream.

For Dumitru Tsepeneag, too, the paradoxical superiority of the reader over the writer resides in "his permanent virtuality," and for the haughty writer, on the other hand, reading might become a form of redemption through humility and human solidarity with the Other. In the space of reading what occurs is a virtual encounter with the anonymous reader, who lacks the author's exhibitionism in producing, ultimately, only simulacra of authentic creation. Beyond the usual intellectual curiosity, the writer confesses his desire, one that is not in the least literary, to reach the other, fragile being, his fellow man, whom he supposes, however, not to be obsessed with the vocation of becoming an Author, or with the mania to "stage" a creation (as in the remarkable short story "Înscenare" ["A Staging"] by the same Tsepeneag): "I read not so much from curiosity as much as from a discipline of humility, in order thereby to reach, in spite of the often deceptive and always parricidal work, my fellow man, who is left on the outside, on the cover. It is an attempt at solidarity with him, who is just as hypocritical and as desperate as myself, just as un-free, just as mortal."[31] The un-freedom and desperation of waiting in hypocrisy—attenuated, in the political and cultural context of socialist realism, only by the situation of going against the grain of ideological censorship—could find its

31 Dumitru Ţepeneag, "Laudă anonimului" [Laus anonymi], in *Momentul oniric*, 106.

compensation in lucid control over the oneiric text. But also in the solidarity of the literary group, based on like-mindedness and subversive self-definition in relation to political power. A suspect solidarity, of course, in the eyes of the one-party state, as long as the manifestos and polemics of the oneirics sometimes even invoked a broader communal solidarity of writers with readers. According to the model of the privileged complicity of the writer with his fellow man wherever he might be—*the reader*—the solidarity of those equally "un-free" seemed designed to be achieved at some point also outside their literary group.

In "Autorul şi personajele sale" ["The Author and His Characters"], Dumitru Tsepeneag constructs more than merely a subtle essay on the aesthetics of the modern novel of Joyce, Kafka, and Robbe-Grillet, viewed in relation to the "traditional" novel of Balzac and Zola. Frequently, and therefore symptomatically, throughout his argument, Tsepeneag the novelist-essayist suggests, without explicitly formulating it, an insidious link between a certain choice of narrative viewpoint and power relations within the social agora. It is precisely these relations that the micro-universe of the novel mythologizes and thereby amplifies, conferring upon them ontological legitimacy. Firstly, when he analyzes the pride of the omniscient and omnipotent novelist demiurge, Tsepeneag concludes that the illusion of power held by the author is also transmitted to the reader: "The reader is happy alongside the author, as though at the right hand of the Father. Happy in knowing everything, understanding everything. He is the author's special guest in this marvelous domain of reality, where he meets people like himself and like his neighbor, but to whom he is evidently superior. He is above them and within them, he knows all their habits, manias, vices (. . .) What is created in this way is a complicity between author and reader, which causes the latter not only to be happy, but also grateful."[32] The paterfamilias or, even more so, "master of slaves" authority of the realist and naturalist novelist, for whom the world is his "penal colony," leads to an *Oedipal condition* on the part of the character, argues Tsepeneag. His fate is thus decided by the textual god, who determines that he should be life-like, adding to his mimetic writing even certain deformities, whether didactic or ideological, out of the need, I might add, to persuade and even control the reader and reception of the text. It is a will to power similar to that of the political, almost a compulsive desire to gain additional control over the attitude of the receptor. What is at stake is to monitor, in the case of the audience-receptor, the aesthetic and extra-aesthetic reaction, the latter also being influenced by the human model provided by the aesthetic canon. The opinion according to which the reader might nevertheless be happy, even grateful, allowing himself to be manipulated by the Author and his almost inviolable authority, seems to be a remark that is sooner bitterly ironic on Tsepeneag's part. For it was the same reader that was manipulated by aesthetic authority, just as he was manipulated, sometimes with depressing ingenuity, by political authority.

*

The character is an Oedipus within his forewritten destiny, a destiny without exit, and the reader, seated "at the right hand of the Father,"

32 D. Ţepeneag, "Autorul şi personajele sale" [The Author and His Characters], in *Viaţa românească*, no. 5, 1967, 128.

the genuinely omnipotent author, receives the drug of illusory omnipotence, he is content to "applaud" the performance. "But is the reader not also a kind of Oedipus, the same as the character?" we might ask ourselves today, reading this essay from Tsepeneag's youth. The break with this state of affairs, with realist literature (and, moreover, with socialist realism, which brought with it the demand to convey an ethical, ideologically correct message), supervenes through the subjectivization and relativization of the position of authority held by His Highness the Author. What has occurred is "an apparently insignificant fact, but which has proved to have incalculable consequences: the author has begun to write about himself,"[33] having had the revelation, as a character himself, that he does not know his own destiny, with the hidden crannies of the subconscious and all, often acting subversively against the character on the surface. Stendhal was the first to exploit this "shared introspection," and the *authentic*, that which is at stake in such a literature, finds itself at odds with the *lifelike*, as Tsepeneag grasps, with the accuracy of essayistic distinctions.

According to the oneiric prose writer and essayist, this is how the questions that arise before an author in a crisis of creative identity might sound. In parallel, the author also undergoes a cognitive crisis and a crisis of power: "If he does not even know himself, is not his knowledge of the other then artificial? Knowledge of the man in the street, whom he forces to become a character, depriving him of his freedom in exchange for an outline, a character, a destiny."[34] At the time when Tsepeneag was writing this essay, in

33 Ibid., 129.

34 Ibid.

those years of the fleeting "springtime," of the brief and deceptive period of post-Stalinist and post-socialist-realist liberalization under Ceauşescu, the Author of destiny was sooner the political Father, the single party, more than the writer. And even less so the oneiric and textualist writer, whose precarious freedom constantly had to be negotiated with Power.[35] In his position as master of slaves, the author, gradually reduced to first-person soliloquies, became an errant knight, in a prose of memory and the search for lost time, and with Kafka and the nouveau roman he is no longer "a mere land surveyor, a topographic engineer aimlessly searching, lost in a world that no longer submits to him, among objects which he wishes to be stripped of any meaning and which he gazes at through a magnifying glass, long and obstinately."[36]

The character becomes anonymous, metamorphosing into a host of chaotic mental motions, tropisms, reified infra-beings. Confronted with the disappearance of characters, as the traditional mainstays of the epic, and the dissemination of the epic itself, the reader, increasingly suspicious of the author's power and authority, and more hesitant in himself, is in search of a new drug. He will

35 In the monograph he dedicates to the work of Dumitru Tsepeneag, Romanian critic Marian Victor Buciu analyzes the resistance of the oneiric theorist and writer to left-wing politics, even after his departure to Paris, in 1971: "He rejects the Trojan horse of the political. He aspires to a purely literary Parisian seduction. However, he knows that the political is part of the curse of modern destiny. He attempts, without false modesty, to resist its evidence. His lucidity once again signals his precarious position: the avant-garde has always been a left-wing business. The extreme left produces in him a revulsion transferred also to the natural left, which is so often naïve or complicitous." *Ţepeneag între onirism, textualism, postmodernism* [*Tsepeneag between Oneiricism, Textualism, Postmodernism*] (Craiova, Editura Aius, 1998), 5.

36 D. Ţepeneag, "Autorul şi personajele sale," 130.

find it in the detective novel or in some other derivative formula, whose authors have encyclopedic pretensions, "honest craftsmen" to whom the demiurgic epic appears merely a trade. The old conventions are held in great honor, and the easily manipulatable characters remain in slavery. And this is in order that the reader shall not be programmatically unsettled, but rather return to his comfortable armchair, from where he will happily applaud. In his argument, Tsepeneag resorts to the metaphor of theatricality, finding the solution of relating the author to characters and readers in the model of the theatrical and performing arts. Whereas the character, to allude to Pirandello, needs an author in order to exist, in order to be able to perform his living drama, the author cannot renounce the character "in order to make himself heard and believed by the reader," as both are free in relation to each other, each recognizing the autonomous existence of the Other.

The rhetorical question, the same as hope, which becomes rhetorical in a period of ideologically controlled literature, persists and was to persist still for a few decades. It can be reread and reinvested today with a meaning it did not explicitly possess at the time. Therefore, it may, of course, be politicized by means of a retrospective interpretation, one that is at once "suspicious" and empathetic, or at the least it may read in an ethical key. Tsepeneag's soundings and dilemmas, like those of any other writer whose texts were at the time preserved free of infection by propagandistic theses, is today interesting not so much at an exclusively aesthetic and literary-typological level as much as at the level of ethics and mentality: "Who knows? Perhaps in the end the Author will resign himself and admit that the relationship between himself and his character is one between two free persons, like between a director and an actor."[37] Naturally, the Author of the Stalinist and Ceauşescu periods was frequently one and the same with the ideological Father, with Power, and then the subjugated or merely duplicitous victim, tyrannized into accepting a pre-determined destiny, into verifying a schema, was both the writer-character and the reader. Their roles were also akin due to hypocritical options for self-preservation, due to half-freedoms, sometimes due to subversion, sometimes due to freely accepted self-censorship. A mise en abyme of guilt experienced by the author-character towards his creation, or, to be more precise, towards the living nightmare produced by his own gaze, which makes murders and other almost indescribable horrors become phantasmal, can be found in the short poetic prose piece entitled "Heautontimoroumenos. Bocet pe o aceeaşi temă" ["Heautontimoroumenos. Lamentation on a Single Theme"], dating from 1969. To a lesser extent than the earlier textualist novella "A Staging" (analyzed more closely in a later chapter of this essay), the "lamentation" of "Heautontimoroumenos" reveals the inextricable link between Oneiricism and textualism, as methods of discursive generation and structuring. The textual demiurge is the one who gives birth to the text *as if he were dreaming it*, so that the prose piece is constructed as a spatiotemporal continuum (also conveyed by means of the graphic continuum of endless sentences and paragraphs beginning with small letters), and draws upon oneiric legislation: "everything recommences from the beginning the victims are dragged once more over the snow whiter and whiter shining brighter by the street lamp whose light becomes

37 Ibid.

ever stronger as the slaughter goes on (. . .) I know precisely that I shall see the same unbearably horrific scenes and then who is to blame who is truly guilty the author of this never-ending massacre if not I myself."

Thanks to the fascination of the lucid and apparently free position of the subject (the narrator or "director" of the performance in the poems of Dimov, for example), as well as to the presupposed empathetic reader, Oneiricism nevertheless offered much more than a fictional palliative. It offered a model for exciting group complicity, one that was primarily aesthetic. Lucid control of the literary construct is one of the main points of the aesthetics of 1960s Oneiricism, to which the Cluj "neo-oneirics" Ruxandra Cesereanu and Corin Braga relate polemically. While Ruxandra Cesereanu argues for "deliriumism" and for oneiric, innate and instinctual trance, Corin Braga inclines (in a provocative confrontation of ideas between himself and Tsepeneag in 1992[38]) toward "hallucinatory, empathetic Oneiricism," toward the authentically phantasmagoric and toward the "anarchetypes" of the universal imagination, which he launches in a manifesto with comparativist accents. Referring on the other hand to the way in

38 See Corin Braga, "Halucinatoria. Resurecția onirismului" [The Resurrection of Oneiricism], in *România literară*, no. 6, 26 February–4 March 1992, 4; Corin Braga, "Onirism estetic şi onirism halucinatoriu" [Aesthetic Oneiricism and Hallucinatory Oneiricism], in *România literară*, no. 21, 28 July–4 August 1992, 4; see also Dumitru Țepeneag, "Scamat(e)oria. Cu sapa într-o mînă şi jobenul în cealaltă" [Sleight of Hand {with a pun in Romanian on "theory"}. With a Mattock in one Hand and a Top-hat in the other], in *România literară*, no. 13, 14–22 April 1992, 4, where he reaffirms that the oneirics placed the emphasis on the mechanism of the dream and not on the raw material provided by it, inasmuch as for them the dream constituted not "a source of images, but rather a criterion, the legislative model.

which, according to Ion Barbu's model of poetic geometry, Leonid Dimov sublimates the phantasmic matter of the dream into ideas and lucidly subjects it to oneiric legislation, Corin Braga discovers as a psychoanalytical argument a biographical trauma of identity suffered by the author of *Cartea de vise* [*The Book of Dreams*]. The reason why Dimov would not give himself up to oneiric trances, even though he was hypnotized by them, but rather left the lamp of consciousness burning was, according to Corin Braga, as follows: "Like a child frightened by the apparitions of the dark, the poet seems desirous to fall asleep with the lamp burning in the chamber of his art. The reason for this combined attraction toward but fear of the revelations of sleep might be found in a devastating childhood trauma, which drew a curtain between the compartments of the poet's soul. It is a question of the failed marriage between his mother, Nadia Dimov, and father, Naum Mordcovici. The son of a Romanian mother and a Jewish father, Leonid deeply felt all the avatars of the extremely anti-Semitic mentality of pre-War Romania. The external ideological pressure, assimilated to the laws of a dictatorial super-ego, led not only to the break-up of his parents' marriage, but also to an inner rupture in the young Leonid. The 'feminine,' maternal imagination found itself cleft by the 'masculine,' paternal lucidity."[39] But the oneirics' desire to evade the accusation of escapism and to *invade* in their turn an already ideologically "occupied" reality, as well as their strategy of remaining vigilant against the attacks of ideological censorship, were stronger motives for the recourse to lucidity than any trauma of identity retrospectively analyzable through

39 Corin Braga, "Poezia lui Leonid Dimov între Oneiros și Logos" [The Poetry of Leonid Dimov between Oneiros and Logos], in *Euphorion*, no. 1–2, January–February 2004, 8.

Freudian or Lacanian psychoanalysis. As for the fact that the oneiricists rejected as naïve the method of calquing only the oneiric phantasmagorical, let me point out that Dimov—as well as Tsepeneag—saw in the disordered transposition of the dream flux into text nothing more than another naturalist method of writing, which he viewed polemically and even condescendingly.

The solidarity within the oneiric group was to a certain extent politicized. This politicization of the movement came about in the sense of aiming a number of polemical arrows from oneiric poetics at the tenets of the July Theses and the clichés promoted by socialist realism. As Tsepeneag confesses, on being challenged by Ion Simuț: "In fact, it was I who consciously politicized the oneiric movement. Dimov reproached me for it from the very start. I didn't know whether he was right . . . But at the time I was convinced that this was the only way we would be able to create a strong enough impact to get ourselves noticed and to promote our literature."[40] It was thus a complicity based on strategies for gaining public visibility and on affinities in stylistic and theoretical choices, untainted by the pseudo-cultural sickness of socialist-realist ideology.

*

In a provocative and substantial collection of essays about the relationship between literature and politics in the intellectual history of the twentieth century, entitled *Modernitatea ultimă* [*The Final Modernity*], Caius Dobrescu argues for the paradoxical convergence between aesthetic and political radicalism. The

40 Dumitru Țepeneag, *Clepsidra răsturnată*, 101.

avant-gardes ultimately contain many theses of aggressive and even totalitarian ideology. The Surrealist, Expressionist, and Futurist manifestos were, as is well known, contiguous with either left-wing or right-wing totalitarianism. After the de-Stalinizing "thaw" of the 1960s, the neo-avant-gardists maintained merely a formal subversion and even self-subversion, much less aggressive than that of their predecessors, rather "an outburst of the anarchic side of revolutionary ideology."[41] A certain degree of anarchism, understood as a temperamental/artistic option, perhaps one that was slightly bovarist, and in any case lacking in any doctrinaire rigor, was also characteristic of the young Tsepeneag, for example, even according to his own confessions.

In this context, that of the self-assertion of the counter-culture, both in the West and in the East, in spite of the peculiarities of the police state in the communist bloc countries, Oneiricism appears in the Romania of the 1970s as a subversion against authority and the official cultural propaganda, on the one hand, and as programmatically situated against the grain of the left-wing surrealism of Breton and Aragon of the previous decades. With the additional nuance that Breton's model of aesthetic radicalism, which for the French surrealist also had an ideological springboard, nevertheless seems acceptable to Tsepeneag as a formula for *political provocation*, but not as a poetics of pure psychical automatism, devoid of controlling reason. On the other hand, Dumitru Tsepeneag accepted the association of aesthetic "doctrine" between oneiric prose and surrealist painting, as he has

41 Caius Dobrescu, *Modernitatea ultimă. Eseuri* [*Late Modernity. Essays*] (Bucharest: Editura Univers, 1998), 109.

frequently affirmed it and transposed it in what might be called his *picto-texts*.

Ultimately, had André Breton's thesis about the absence of rational and ethical control over automatic writing been published in the Romania of the Stalinist or Ceauşescu period, it would have been of such a nature as to encourage the totalitarian abuse of power.[42] In 1968, in the article "Preamble" published in *Luceafărul* magazine, Leonid Dimov quoted Lenin, via André Breton, in connection with the revolutionary political position of Surrealism: "Revolutionary and pragmatic by definition, Surrealism—strangely enough—resorts to automatic writing, setting out from Lenin's imperative: 'We must dream!'"[43] What is interesting is the parallel that Dimov implicitly makes, on the one hand, between the "petit bourgeois," as the type of the eternal philistine, against whom the aesthetic and ideological defiance of his surrealist forebears was directed, and the censors and propagandists of the communist regime, on the other. Both the petits bourgeois and the post-Stalinist communists of the 1970s found themselves in the position of condemning art— be it too revolutionary, be it decadent—that conspired against what both the one and the other claimed to

42 The thesis with regard to the ideological manipulation of the reader through the works of the surrealist avant-garde, which is often imbued with totalitarian thinking, is reiterated by Caius Dobrescu: "The reader presupposed by a certain kind of text has no contract with the authorial authority that issues the text. He might, hypothetically speaking, be subjected to any abuse, to any change in code, register, context. The contract, if one indeed exists, is that he must completely surrender to the 'initiator,' as in certain rites of passage. But even this neophytic aura cannot hide the fact that the ideal reader of a surrealist manifesto, for example, is a humbled and humiliated reader" (101).

43 Leonid Dimov, "Preambul," in *Momentul oniric*, 35.

be "reality." The former disavowed Surrealism, while the latter, the Romanian communists of 1968–1971, viewed Oneiricism with suspicion, the same as they did non-ideologized artistic experimentation in general, imputing to it the sin of escapism and exclusivist intolerance, of aesthetic autism and elitism.

Deploring the prejudice that in the domain of oneiric poetry Hypnos supposedly reigned supreme and rejecting the accusation of escapism and subversion of the status quo (decided by the single-party state) leveled at the oneirics, Dimov argues that "we ought to agree with the Surrealists' indomitable aversion toward the petit bourgeois."[44] Later, the same Dimov amicably reproached Tsepeneag for endangering the existence of the oneiric group in order to satisfy his desire to be in political opposition. In his conversations with Ion Simuţ, Dumitru Tsepeneag invokes this amicable quarrel with Dimov and formulates the following explanation and retrospective justification for his attitude, one that is conscious of its own relativity: "He [i.e. Dimov] was right to a certain extent, because I wasn't doing it [i.e. politicizing Oneiricism] for the sake of Goma (who was rather a pretext). I was doing it, let's say, for two reasons, which, I think, were connected. In the first place, to fight against the regime I hated, for all kinds of motives, including autobiographical. And, implicitly, against the censors, which is to say, not only against political censorship, but also the aesthetic censorship that at the beginning of the 1960s was still strong. The second reason was more selfish and more literary at the same time. We had to draw attention to ourselves somehow or other . . . The simplest way to attract attention, as I explained to

44 Ibid.

Dimov, was for us to dare to do what others didn't dare. For us to provoke the adversary. My model, as regards political provocation, was French Surrealism, the activity of the likes of Breton, whom Dimov didn't love."[45]

It seems that Dumitru Tsepeneag opted not for aesthetic escapism but for subversion and even political provocation, of the kind formerly practiced by Breton (but without him sharing the political colors of most of the Surrealists). The Oneiricism practiced and theorized by Tsepeneag would be processed and re-written into an original synthesis, with a lucid awareness of intertextuality, felt to be necessary and creative, and with the methods of textual construction provided by the nouveau roman and the incipient textualism of precursors such as Raymond Roussel.[46] It is difficult to speak of synchronization only at the aesthetic level with the literary movements of the West without taking into account a number of paradoxes of the incidence between the sphere of the literary and that of the political in the 1960s and '70s. Surely the interaction of writing with Power ought to be approached today, within a new literary-political history, from an ethical perspective that is understanding

45 Dumitru Țepeneag, *Clepsidra răsturnată*, 121.

46 Ibid., 127: "The surrealists believed that if they put themselves into as unconscious a state as possible they would manage to see the dream again or at least a part of the images in the dream. Naïveté! In fact, the dream does not reside in images that are in any case evanescent, but rather in the textual operations that they enact or merely suggest in its poietic mechanism . . . The method of authentic oneiricism is textualist, i.e. auto-deiegetic . . . Textualism, as I conceive it, has an incontestable precursor, which Romanian theorists or writers concerned with theory do not seem to recognize except very vaguely, and namely Raymond Roussel, who lived and wrote before the Second World War."

toward the Other, toward fellow man, whether author or reader, subject to the times, and therefore manipulatable to a greater or lesser degree, regardless of which side of the Iron Curtain he was on? Otherwise, as the history of the twentieth century has demonstrated, often tragically, it is not only writing that is in the service of power (of course, this was a well-known situation in Romania, with the authors of propagandistic literature and "homages" before 1989), but also the one who writes possesses and "practices," or stages, through the very act of writing, a form of power or Power itself.[47] And the struggles for power pit various kinds of writing against each other, or, as Jacques Derrida puts it, "*les* luttes pour *les* pouvoirs oppossent *des* écritures." For, what are the rewriting and ideologization of history,[48] its distortion depending on the interests of a particular moment, of a given society, other than a terrible and often dangerous form of wielding

47 Caius Dobrescu argues for the "guilt" of a large part of literature under communism, in particular that of the novel of "the obsessive decade," for having fallen into the trap of complicity with Power and even an amoral fascination with it, in this way becoming incapable of providing any alternative to the ideological discourse: "In the 1960s, all over Eastern Europe the possibility emerged for the transformation of the novel into a discourse alternative to that of power. In Romania, however, this did not mean an orientation toward values which today we have defined as belonging to civil society. When it genuinely saw itself as an alternative, literature offered itself not as a mere privileged ancillary, as in the cases discussed above, but rather as an emulator of power. The novel of 'the obsessive decade' is rarely an analysis of totalitarianism. Its dominant is a terrible fascination with the idea of Power. The Romanian writer did not set out to demystify the popular phantasm of the ubiquity of this power. His sensibility quickly pushed him into a very strange kind of envy" (175).

48 See Richard Schechner, *Performance Studies. An Introduction* (London and New York: Routledge, 2002), 126: "All writing enacts agendas of power. Writing doesn't serve power, but the other way around: who writes performs authority."

power over the other, of manipulating and "cannibalizing" that Other, along with the non-recognition of his difference and his abusive political regimentation?

It is necessary to analyze the political context, full of revolutionary enthusiasm and infused with a pro-Marxist mentality, among many intellectuals in the West, as well as the extremely complex context of the communist East, thronged with the illusions of a temporary thaw, first after the Prague Spring and then, in Romania, with the subversion and even opposition of a number of writers, including the oneiricist Tsepeneag (also a supporter of Paul Goma), to the totalitarian system, which had in any case only just emerged from Stalinism and socialist realism. It is also necessary to add, in connection with the western affinities of Dumitru Tsepeneag, that both the Tel Quel group and some nouveau roman authors had clear left-wing sympathies and displayed, if not always a radical attitude toward traditional literature and literary theory, then at least an albeit implicit critical attitude toward the capitalist system, political and bureaucratic power, and the market economy. This critical attitude was also aimed at human alienation and reification (going as far as the infra-character and tropes of the nouveau roman). The inner attitude of the young "anarchist" Tsepeneag (as he sometimes called himself, with ironic detachment) was nevertheless based, in the case of his opting for the prose of Robbe Grillet or Robert Pinget, not on political-literary sympathies or divergences, but on poetic and ontological correspondences in creation, on correspondences in textuality, imagery and style. In a conversation from 1990 with Alain Robbe-Grillet, whose novels *Les Gommes* and *Dans le labyrinthe* Dumitru Tsepeneag had translated during the Ceauşescu period, the two writers debate, among other things, the well-known relationship between socialist, Marxist revolution and literary revolution:

> R.-G. You know, as soon as my books began to be of interest to young people, to students in particular, at the end of the 1960s, and I was invited to give lectures or even seminars, well, the universities that invited me were always marked by Marxism or left-wing politics. I mean to say that in the "well-behaved" universities, where no one was thinking about socialist revolution, no one was thinking about literary revolution either. I wasn't a communist, I couldn't even be considered a "man of the left," but I was still invited for the spirit of intellectual adventure that was felt in my work.
>
> D.Ț. *All right, but you did also have admirers on the other side. For example, like other intellectuals from the East, I was not a communist, and had even suffered personally because of the socialist revolution, but nevertheless your literary work and the nouveau roman in general were immediately attractive to me. It was more or less a direction in which I too had been trying to move, in spite of the obstacles the so-called communist regime placed in front of the avant-garde.*[49]

49 Dumitru Țepeneag, "Marxismul e pe ducă, alte pericole ne pîndesc" [Marxism is on the way out, other dangers stalk us] (in conversation with Alain Robbe-Grillet), in *Reîntoarcerea fiului la sînul mamei rătăcite* [*The Son's Return to the Bosom of the Errant Mother*] (Jassy: Editura Institutul European, 1993), 14.

Postmodernism, together with its "university" ideology, post-structuralism, which was also more often than not left-wing, seems to provoke a skeptical reaction not only in Tsepeneag but also in his celebrated French interlocutor. In any case, Robbe-Grillet deplores the lack of interest on the part of younger writers in discovering the *new*, as a value in itself, and evokes, by contrast, the "revolutionary" impetus of the 1960s generation, the belief in human and hence literary progress, combined with the desire for social freedom, which then, in 1990, seemed to have been dispersed: "Simon, Duras and myself were always anticommunists. In spite of that, we believed in a kind of human progress linked to the advance of literature, which had to bring additional social freedom. Whereas they [i.e. younger writers such as Echenoz, Toussaint, Marie Redonnet, and Deville] don't seem to believe in that. They have a kind of modesty, a gentleness that disturbs me. We took a pride in our work."[50] Indeed, the exasperation of this "pape du nouveau roman" with the postmodern author is explicable, because the latter no longer has the modernist (often elitist, I might add) pride of the demiurge that his creative work presupposes, but seems to repeat, with a certain nonchalance and even humility, the work of his predecessors. Sometimes, the latter even succumbs to parody or voluntary pastiche of previous texts out of an *ethical* intention to rewrite the cultural canon of the past, which itself is felt to be oppressive and totalitarian.

A correct radiography of the frequently twinned political and literary implications of Oneiricism can be achieved only by grasping and decanting its sinuous relations, both at the aesthetic

50 Ibid., 16.

and cultural level more broadly, with modernism and the historic avant-garde, and then with Romanian neo-modernism, centered on resistance through culture and on the return to the aesthetic during an epoch otherwise dominated by socialist realism. Finally, what should also be brought into discussion are the contiguities as well as the divergent nuances of Oneiricism in relation to the counter-culture and "alternative" art of the 1960s and aesthetic postmodernism, but also in relation to political and ethical postmodernism, which is bound to post-structuralist ideology, derived from the French revolt of the 1960s against "structuralism" and from sympathy with the student insurrections of 1968. In addition, today, any reconsideration of the adversarial relationship between Oneiricism and socialist realism needs to be carried out by means of a prospective, or retro-prospective, to be more exact, comparison of the oneiric movement with the Romanian textualism of the 1980s (and with the other side of the literary and meta-textual model in Romanian literature—the Tîrgovişte School), as well as with European resonances and synchronisms (Euro-centric but also sometimes Euro-skeptic) with the nouveau roman and the literature of the absurd in the vein of Kafka, Beckett, and even Ionesco.

*

Today, with a retrospective analysis of the literary past in the ideological context of the final decades of totalitarianism, it becomes increasingly clear that this canon, justified by means of "purist," aesthetic arguments, was contaminated and willingly accepted by the Party, and was situated ambiguously between the underground counter-culture and the official cultural discourse. In the alternative list of Romanian writers *outside the canon* before 1989 can be recognized, among others, Leonid Dimov, Mircea Ivănescu, and Mircea Horia Simionescu. The question is whether here, in an abundantly aesthetic and biographical dynamic posture, always in the vanguard of anti-realist theory and prose, it is also possible to place Dumitru Tsepeneag, the bilingual neo-avant-garde writer and founder, alongside Leonid Dimov, of a literary group, the ideologue and theorist of structural Oneiricism, then the representative and inspired parodist of the nouveau roman (in *Arpièges/Zadarnică e arta fugii* [*Vain Art of the Fugue*]), the textualist novelist in a battle with his own linguistic exile (in *Pigeon vole/Porumbelul zboară! . . .* [*Pigeon Post*] and *Le Mot sablier/Cuvîntul nisiparniță* [*The Sandglass Word*]), the narrative film director of a self-referential cinematic scenario (*Roman de gare/Roman de citit în tren* [*Novel for Reading on the Train*]), and the author of an exceptional trilogy or even tetralogy of Romanian cultural identity and European identity more broadly (*Hotel Europa, Pont des Arts, Maramureș, La belle Roumaine*), in which comparative imagology, ironic politology, and the parody of the oneiric discourse do not exclude a mythologizing vision of our Mioritic "matrix."

Pertaining to *anti-canonical* eternity, as well as the aesthetic anti-canon and the anti-canon of subversive cultural ideology, the dynamic fictional and biographical identity of Țepeneag/Tsepeneag/Pastenague has prompted recent literary history to confront once again its own organic demand. Having existed for such a long time, without, however, being fully taken into account in the post-communist space, the need for this history to rethink at last its outmoded criteria of value brings with it another, equally acute demand: that of reopening once and for all the debate (with aesthetic, ethical, political and perhaps even resentful arguments, in the sense of the well-known *school of resentment*) about the need for a canon of alternative literature.

II.

FICTIONAL IDENTITY AND ONEIRIC IMAGOLOGY

Distortion of the psychology, typology, and conventions of the realist character • Rendering fictional figures anonymous • The oneiric infra-character and nouveau roman tropes • The de-anthropomorphized double • The split "I" and its zoomorphic and mechanomorphic projections • An eccentric typology: the angel-dandy • The aestheticism of the angelic character • *The Wait*—quasi-mystical dream and the aesthetic strategy of textual generation

As a theoretician—alongside Leonid Dimov, in particular—of the Oneiricism of the 1960s and '70s, Dumitru Tsepeneag detects the ancestry of this type of literature not in the doctrine of automatic writing, but in Surrealist painting, which juxtaposes images within a paradoxical spatiotemporal simultaneity. The anticipated effect at the literary level was "a kind of painted music, of time ceaselessly converted into space" ("The Oneiric Endeavor, after the War"[51]). Seeing in the dream merely a criterion or legislative

51 Leonid Dimov, Dumitru Ţepeneag, *Momentul oniric*, 219.

model, aesthetic Oneiricism signifies a lucid textual construct and "has the ambition of reconciling Breton with Valéry."[52] The textualism of the Eighties Generation here exists, in seed, not only in the sense of self-referentiality, but also in that of a magnificent engendering of the text, which sets out from multiple vanishing points and from a harmoniously handled parodic technique (as in Tsepeneag's novels *Vain Art of the Fugue* and *The Necessary Marriage*). Dumitru Tsepeneag's affiliation to "the anti-realist, literary and meta-literary paradigm" of Romanian literature is, in the opinion of Gheorghe Crăciun,[53] an evident literary-historical fact. In any case for Crăciun, a prose writer and theoretician of the Eighties Generation, the Tîrgoviște School, Oneiricism and, lastly, the epic postmodernism of the 1980s are three distinct facets of the same paradigm.

Emerging in the midst of an *era of suspicion* toward the traditional epic discourse, the quasi-textualist Oneiricism of *Așteptarea* [*The Wait*] (as well as that of the author's previous volumes, *Exerciții* [*Exercises*] (1966) and *Frig* [*Cold*] (1967)) adopts so-called objectivity, anti-psychologism, and an apparently neutral, "anonymous" style, as well as a preference for the hallucinatory, esoteric detail. These are also attributes of the French nouveau roman, to which Tsepeneag had been receptive from the very first. The characters of the short stories and, often, the later novels of Dumitru Tsepeneag agglutinate gradually, tentatively, as fictional entities that are conventionally anti-psychological, anonymous and often rendered unreal. This is why their passage into the possible order of *as if* will

52 Ibid.

53 *Cu garda deschisă* [*With Guard Lowered*] (Jassy: Editura Institutul European, 1997), 55.

sometimes be metaphorically transposed through an affiliation with a strange, hybrid, often non-human, realm of being.

The writer's option for characters that express a type of non-human subjectivity has polemical motivations. It contains, in fact, a number of fertile nuclei for a polemical vision of the human, specific to late modernism. Tsepeneag synchronizes, involuntarily and as a result more authentically, with the theories of *posthumanity* of recent decades. The "human, all too human" condition of subjectivity and traditional affectivity in contemporary theoretical discourse, descended from the "masters of suspicion" (Nietzsche, Marx, Freud) and from the cultural archaeology of Michel Foucault, is rethought as *posthuman*. The metaphor from Foucault's *Les mots et les choses*, according to which the human is dead, and has left nothing more than a footprint in the sand, at the edge of the sea, re-inscribes the terrible, likewise metaphorical, verdict of Nietzsche regarding the death of God.

Hermeneuticist Stanley Cavell, for example, considers that the "present" of the final decades of the twentieth century was dominated by a *post-romantic, post-subjective* form of civilization—a phenomenon also certainly noticeable today, at the beginning of the twenty-first century—"in which nothing that happens any longer strikes us as the objectification of subjectivity, as the act of an answerable agent, as the expression and satisfaction of human freedom, of human intention and desire."[54] And for the theoreticians

54 The following is the paragraph in which Cavell characterizes post-romantic and post-subjective civilization: "Is this new [romantic, subjective] form of civilization being replaced by another [i.e., post-romantic, post-subjective]? In particular, is it being replaced by one in which nothing that happens any longer strikes us as the objectification of subjectivity, as the act of an answerable agent, as the expression and satisfaction of human freedom, of human intention and

of virtual hyperreality, *posthumanity*[55] presupposes the dematerialization of information and the construction of a type of *cyborg*, as a technological artifact—a veritable cultural icon, in fact, of the epoch of virtual postmodernity. Thus, the fact that we are becoming "posthumans" is due, according to Katherine Hayles, to the growing importance that the informational mold is acquiring to the detriment of the material. The human psyche is ineluctably metamorphosing, given that the body itself is coming to be seen as a replaceable prosthesis, in which the biological receives mechanical characteristics and is situated within a bio-cybernetic ensemble. The new post-subjective or trans-subjective ontology naturally also re-dimensions the condition of literary creativity. At the level of textual virtuality, the book ought to adopt the materiality of its specific medium, of its means of communication, respectively a

---

desire? What has a beginning can have an end. If this future (civilization?) were effected its members would not be dissatisfied. They would have lost the concept of satisfaction. Then nothing would (any longer) give them the idea that living beings, human things, could feel. So they would not (any longer) be human." See Stanley Cavell, *The Claim of Reason: Wittgenstein, Skepticism, Morality, and Tragedy* (New York: Oxford University Press, 1979), 468. For Cavell, romanticism is, from the philosophical point of view, an emblem of "subjectivism," but also of the ontology of the human, seen as the opposite of the monstrous. No longer to be human presupposes the abandonment of the subjective perspective and the revelation of "horror," of the monstrous. The end of the romantic episteme means "the vanishing of the human." The reification of subjectivity, of the human, brings with it, for Cavell, a paradoxical next self, an oblique subjectivity, which no longer defines itself in relation to transcendental knowledge. This future I undermines any fixed, metaphysical interpretation of the very idea of subjectivity. The I takes shape as a project on the way to fulfilment, as possessing an I is no longer the possession of a self, but a "process of moving to, and from, nexts" (Ibid., 12).

55 See N. Katherine Hayles, *How We Become Posthuman: Virtual Bodies in Cybernetics, Literature, and Informatics* (Chicago: University of Chicago Press, 1999).

paradoxical *non-materiality* of a virtual type. And the category of the *literary*—which even today still presupposes the preexisting consciousness of a creator, as a liberal-humanist subject, characterized by general, human universality—would consequently acquire a different aesthetic and ontological status. It will have been redimensioned as a continuous creative inter-activity of virtual textualism, centered on methods of cybernetic art: three-dimensional simulation, virtual imagery, fractal models, etc.

In the textualist novel *Pigeon vole*,[56] Dumitru Tsepeneag transcribes, via the words of Ed Pastenague, his double within the fictional frame, the anxiety of the textual creator confronted with the specter of being replaced by a non-subjective creative instance, one that is omnipotent at the virtual level—the computer: "And let's say that they did get rid of written works, and the writer were to come forward, to occupy center stage, to prove himself persuasive, seductive; it's then he would unveil his only secret: his agony. There's a whiff of putrefaction about the writer, he's stinking up the place. No wonder we want him replaced by computers: clean and immortal." In *Pont des Arts*, a palimpsest that rewrites previous novels, the supra-character of the novelist appears to be more and more dependent upon the computer, upon the electronic condition (one that is therefore more fluctuating, more unstable) of his text. The protagonists of the picaresque novel within a novel

56 *Pigeon vole*, written in French under the pseudonym Ed Pastenague, was published in 1989 by Éditions P.O.L; in 1997, was published in Romanian by Editura Univers with the title *Porumbelul zboară! . . .* [*Fly, Pigeon*], "translated," thus rewritten, by D. Ţepeneag. English version, with the title *Pigeon Post*, translated by Jane Kuntz, Champaign, IL & London, Dalkey Archive Press, 2008.

are Vasile from Maramureş (a rural, pastoral region of north-west Romania), Gigi and Ana, but also Fuhrmann and Myoko. The primary fictional world collides with the secondary fictional world. The second, situated in a diaphragmatic, intermediary space, thus with "one foot" in "real" reality, deconstructs the epic convention of the novel written by a narrator, be he Pastenague or some other Ed, a substitute for the textual demiurge: "Vasile once more held his head in his hands and leaned his elbows on the balustrade of the bridge. He stood like that for a number of minutes in a row, his brow toward the islands, but without seeing them, he was looking downward, at the water, and spitting. I am left rather embarrassed, I don't know what to do, how to go on . . . My eyes are aching. I turn down the brightness of the screen." The virtual world of the text and of the novelistic imagery, which hypnotizes the viewer, simultaneously the character and the internal reader, tends also to swallow up its creator, substituting for him the translucent, shallow, surface reality of the *screen*. It is an anamorphic screen, eternally glittering reflectively and, ultimately, eternally illusionistic, with an extra-textual reference that is just as illusory. Elsewhere, in *Roman de citit în tren* [*Novel for Reading on the Train*], the director, who there appears as a true demiurge of the fictional act, also forgets to turn off "the now-blank screen." The ghostliness of the computer screen, emptied of content, of referentiality, or else endowed with a substance that is par excellence illusory, virtual, also exercises a perverse hypnosis over the Pirandello-like writer-character of hypertexts at the end of *Pont des Arts*:

> "I've finished the book," repeated Marianne . . .
> "I've finished it and I enjoyed it, you know."

> I interrupt myself once again. To be honest, I thought she was talking about *Hotel Europa*. I nod in satisfaction, then I proudly lift my chin, which naturally prevents me from looking at the computer screen. I have the air of a German officer with a monocle. No, I didn't say binoculars, although maybe it would be better to erase it and type binoculars instead of monocle. With those you can see further. And what I see is Pastenague rubbing his hands together behind Fuhrmann.

The proximity of the non-anthropomorphic double, of the virtual demiurge, the computer, has absorbed the subjectivity of the character-author within an *anti-space* or *hyper-space* whose virtuality is friable, constantly undermined by the aggression of the virtual. After he reads the letter addressed to his protagonist, Ana Pânzaru—who reveals his meta-textual condition, even calling him "Dear Author"—the aforementioned "Author" confesses the servitude of his concubinage with the computer: "And so, since I got the computer, I have been looking out of the window less and less . . . The days pass more quickly, life slips away almost without my realizing it, in the silence of the room I hear the whistling or rather the discreet hissing of the computer, and sometimes the light of the screen makes my eyes ache."

The one who utters "I" can be seen to be increasingly menaced by depersonalization, ingested by a trans-subjective, to a certain extent monstrous, force, and by the consequent loss of not only his authority as author, his authorship, but also his ontological identity as humble creature. It seems that his identity exists only insofar as it is performed. And this performativity is a component of his structural theatricality, enacted on a hybrid, fictional/real stage, or even at the boundary between the stage (the novel) and the auditorium (the extra-textual agora).

*

The strongly pictorial quality of Dumitru Tsepeneag's early short stories, in which the images are arranged in a simultaneity, in a spatiotemporal contiguity specific to Surrealist paintings, rather than in the succession specific to the literary discourse, is noticeable as early as the autobiographical prose piece "Amintire" ["Recollection"]. Here, the text abounds in archetypal, or rather stereotypical, images, like faded sepia photographs, in which movement is frozen (see the imperfect aspect of the verbs, suggesting the atemporality of the everyday situations described): "The plump serving girls with their chubby cheeks, dressed in lively colors, would sway in their [i.e. the children's] midst. Stern governesses would scold with uplifted index finger or would tweak an ear as rosy as a petal, which shortly thereafter would forget all sorrow and run off to play. And, *of course* [*emphasis added*], there would also be the comical little dogs . . ." The insertion of the adverbial phrase "of course" accentuates the feeling of déjà vu, of ostentatious artificiality, induced by the apparently pedantic, but in fact ambiguous, description of the images, which are similar to those of a faux-naïve drawing: "And everything, everything would be both far away and close, in a stagnant light, as if you were looking through a window." The specular surface of the window or the mirror signals affective distance, created via memory or the oneiric space, as well as the ambiguity of the oneiric/real boundary, as in the films of Buñuel.

In Victor Brauner's paintings of the *picto-poetry* type, the hybrid, zoomorphic/anthropomorphic or teratological figures can be interpreted as phantasmic doubles of the human subject, framed with its overflowing collective unconscious and all. Somewhat similarly, the short stories of Tsepeneag appear as *ekphrasis*-type discursive renderings of paintings, reproducing the oneiric projections of the "I" and the Other, which is often an animal-man. In *Pigeon vole*, for example, Mme Maryse is constantly walking her little dog Valérie. Beyond the prosaic incident, the compulsive manner in which the scene appears, also repeated as a leitmotif in the novel *Pont des Arts*, might suggest speculations on and associations with the idea of the animal double. As an animated part of the self, its zoomorphic projection and then objectification reveals itself to the "I" in the *waking*, constructed dream.

This ontological *Other*, the animal-man or animal double, appears in Dumitru Tsepeneag's earliest short stories. For example, in "Dedesubt" ["Underneath"], from the volume *Cold*: "It was better as a twosome even though the other had a body covered in harsh fur and sharp canines which it sometimes sank into his shoulder or thigh." Similarly, in "Underneath," in a grotesque oneiric universe dominated by a kind of "mechanical" transcendence, the non-human double is not only zoomorphic but also, and this is something even more alienating, a secret "green eye" in the control panel, or merely that "green, mocking or merely ironic, rarely compassionate, light." Then, in "Plînsul" ["The Weeping"], in the volume *The Wait*, the self's Other, the alien "I," "was neither a vulture nor a lion, because it was weeping. And it was no longer a man, although the dreadfully thin, gaunt body seemed human." In the textual picture that is "Gurru," it might seem that a zoomorphic transcendence is invoked, one that is evil because embittered in its own solitude. Otherwise, if he does not belong to the zone of transcendence, then the character is the inhabitant of a degraded immanence, without any definite metaphysical point of repair. He is a proto-human creature or, more likely, a posthuman creature, a protagonist in a somber futurological fantasy. Although he has the starry heavens above him, no moral law is operative within him any longer: "He is fearful and bad. The glitter of the stars annoys him and their tinkling causes him to shrink back fearfully. On moonlit nights, the up-to-then inert tail lifts up its tip like a viper and swaying angrily lashes the taut beams of light. A strange and sweet music is born. And he takes fright and his slobbering snout trembles. He is so alone and so old . . . Who knows how long his eye with its slightly cracked glass has been dully gazing from up there." The figure of the dreamer in "Gravură" ["Engraving"], having become an itinerant wave-particle through oneiric space-time, is projected in the atemporal, fairy-tale-like fictional silhouette of a "knight." His gaze, in its turn demiurgic, is fastened on movement, which it freezes in the textual "engraving": "At last, the knight returned in haste driving a herd of oxen frightened beneath the blows of the whip. He saw the corpses half covered by large, silver vultures. He dismounted from his horse and, leaning his elbow on the saddle, alone amid the lowing of the frightened oxen and the flapping of the birds, he gazed for a long time unflinching, he gazed absent-mindedly."

In "Ciorile" ["The Crows"], the character loses himself in an ambiguous, grotesque and at the same time fascinating embrace, in a kind of erotic act with an old woman who has been metamorphosed into or doubled by a crow.

The obsessive invocation of, as well as the difficulties of representing, the Other is frequently associated with paradisiacal visions, which seemingly compensate for the highly unstable fracturing of the "I." In the already mentioned short story "Underneath," the "I" menaced by the dictatorial and censoring "green eye" is nostalgic for a simulacrum of paradise glimpsed only for an instant: "He no longer dared to climb the steep stair, to gaze through the crack. And how he longed to glimpse once more the strips of sky and the patches of rosy-bluish skin, to hear the gentle, faraway music and to descry as if through a mist the outlines of dancing creatures." In "Specialistul" ["The Specialist"], a mysterious blotch that appears on the wall miraculously changes colors, like an enchanted kaleidoscope, and is "read" by the protagonist as an occult sign from *beyond*. The humble "specialist" can only "scrape it away" and clarify it for others, but he himself is forbidden to gaze through it. The specialist is merely a helpmeet of the creator, deprived of his creation, merely the intermediary for that animated blotch that he transforms into a magic mirror or into a supra-personal *eye*, intended to capture the gaze of the *chosen*. (The protagonist of the novel *Maramureş* will also be marked with a spot on his shoulder, a sign that he is a *chosen one*, or, contrariwise, a sign of damnation, like the tattoo of a concentration camp prisoner.) The round spot through which, as though in an initiatory, phantasmic scenario, can be glimpsed a kind of paradise seems to be the very objectification or sublimation of the viewing subject within a trans-subjective eye.

The difficult-to-interpret image of this spot or eye might nevertheless be translated as an objectification of a certain hypostasis of the human subject, which contemporary philosopher Slavoj Žižek calls "pure *cogito*." It precisely corresponds, in the opinion of the Slovenian philosopher, "to the fantasy gaze: in it, I found myself reduced to a nonexistent gaze, i.e., after losing all my effective predicates, I am nothing but a gaze paradoxically entitled to observe the world in which I do not exist."[57] The Cartesian *cogito* would therefore possess a status that is sooner imaginary, provided by a specific "self-duplication of the gaze" of the one who thinks of himself as *sum*, as a seemingly weightless *image* of his own experience purified of any particular attributes. In support of his interpretation, Žižek invokes the fantasy Descartes himself transposes in his writings on optics: that of the eye of a dead animal, which man might interpose between himself and reality, thereby observing reality not directly but through the images on the retina of the animal's eye. In the phantasmic spot in Tsepeneag's short story "The Specialist," there is something of the self-duplication of the gaze in the retina of the Other, as an image of the self cleft and successively reintegrated through the ecstasy of the gaze:

> A final scrape of the knife and the specialist's shout of joy! He stepped to one side and cried:
>
> "Place your eye and . . . look!"
>
> Trembling, feeling the wall like a blind man, I pressed my cheek, then my forehead and finally my eyelid against

57 Slavoj Žižek, *Tarrying with the negative: Kant, Hegel, and the Critique of Ideology* (Durham, NC: Duke University Press, 1993), 64.

it. I descried nothing. I was too close, too excited. I turned around, swiveling my gaze in bewilderment. On the bed, the specialist had covered his face with his gnarled red hands. Perhaps he was weeping. When he looked at me, his face was flushed, his gaze fixed.

"Did you see?"

This ecstasy alone, or merely the bovarism of the gaze, transcends the continual and exhausting drama of the self.

In various fantastic compositions by Victor Brauner, bicephalous dragons arranged in a ring, like the mythical Worm Ouroboros, stand alongside anthropomorphic figures or scattered eyes, floating in the waters of oneiric hallucinosis. Likewise, in the important short story "Orașul cu păuni" ["The City with the Peacocks"] by Tsepeneag, the creatures that the "I" gazes upon and describes, with oneiric pedantry, construct an ideogram that has become a calligramme or, ultimately, a hermetic riddle, a cryptogram: "By the wall I descried something red, fleshy, but nevertheless glossy. At first it did not flinch. It seemed to be a snake or an eel. From a corner, another, larger one crawled towards the middle of the room. I could make out the gibbous eye, set at the more swollen end, and seemingly some long, fine threads, like whiskers. It undulated slowly over the floor, heading for the stone bulb on which I was curled up. Why should I have been afraid?"

The phantasmic characters, half indescribable, half "painted" with zoomorphic anatomical details, are endowed, as in the plays of Matei Vișniec (named by Tsepeneag himself as an "oneiric"), with human moods—melancholy, anguish, and even a metaphysical-religious nostalgia for paradise. Most of them are miraculous talking animals, classic protagonists of fables. The micro-prose pieces in "Secvențe naive" ["Naïve Sequences"] are also reminiscent of the short parables or absurdist proverbs of Eugène Ionesco, entitled "Glimmers." But in the work of Dumitru Tsepeneag what dominates is a melancholy and tender attitude toward the bizarre characters, and less the parody omnipresent in Ionesco: "The trainer made his entrance, his boots creaking on the sand. Instead of a whip he had a snake. The lion on my right asked me in a whisper: 'But where is the audience?'" A staging of a naïve-minimalist *circus of the world.*

*

The central character of the oneiric short stories in the volume *The Wait*[58] is also a kind of ontologically intermediate creature, more often than not an angel. In the work of Dumitru Tsepeneag, the angel is particularized by a certain self-consciousness of an aesthetic order. Angelic symbolism, of flight and wings, combined with a programmatic and ostentatious aestheticism, constitutes the royal road of the abyssal poetics of this textualist/oneiric writer. In connection with the bizarre angelic beings that populate short stories such as "Plînsul" ["The Weeping"], "Dor de patrie" ["Homesickness"], "Accidentul" ["The Accident"] and "Așteptare"

58 Published in 1972 (although the date given inside the book is 1971), the volume was withdrawn from the bookshop by the censors. It was not re-published until 1993, also by Editura Cartea Românească. A selection from the first three volumes of short prose by Tsepeneag was published, with the title *Exercices d'attente* by Éditions Flammarion in 1972, translated by Alain Paruit. A new edition, with the title *Attente*, was published by P.O.L in 2003.

["The Wait"], it is possible to speak of a shift in emphasis from the mystic role of the angelic being, the catalyst of human/divine communication and theophanies, toward one that is almost exclusively aesthetic.

Perceived by Rilke under the sign of the aesthetic, the seraphic apparition of The First Duino Elegy represents supernatural, romantic beauty, scornful of the human: "Ein jeder Engel ist schrecklich." The dreadful here represents the almost impossible synthesis of the sublime with the grotesque. It might also be said that the angels in the prose of Dumitru Tsepeneag, with their sooner decadent beauty, are dreadful, involuntarily in line with Rilke. In the short story "Homesickness," the narrator "I" invokes, during an imaginary dialogue with the lover he has abandoned, an angel, his alter ego. The "I" is doubled, projected onto and even confounded with the alter ego, by means of the artifice of the finale, which repeats the beginning and *opens up* the text: the angel has been abandoned in a hotel room full of bedbugs, "he had nothing else to do," he merely contemplates his grimy and ridiculous wings, his top hat, the newspaper, his shoes . . . Consequently, the character/reflector in the prose of Tsepeneag is, it seems, a kind of disabused angel, full of existentialist fatuousness. What we are reading, through a textualist maneuver avant la lettre, are the pages of his indirect diary. This angel refuses to be a vehicle of the divine commandments any more, and his classic insignia, his wings, cease to be functional (in St Augustine and [Pseudo-]Dionysius the Areopagite, angels are defined above all by their *function*), becoming unusable, purely aesthetic. Trembling ambiguously between the natural temptation of *flight*—a favorite motif in Tsepeneag's prose—and its deliberate repression, the wings are more a tragic cry of pride. The one who has tired of mediating between the human and the divine desires, at last, to serve himself, to reveal himself. Precisely for this reason, he makes a show of other emblems of pride: the already mentioned top hat, ostentatiously elegant (also worn by the angel in the short story "The Weeping"), the smoking jacket ("Homesickness," "The Weeping"), the walking cane with a small ivory knob ("The Weeping"), the blue velvet trousers, the lacquered shoes, the buttonhole ("The Accident," "The Weeping," "Homesickness").

The eccentric garb, the suspect, cadaverous pallor, the red, probably dyed hair (the case of the pubescent angel in "The Accident") are not, however, signs of frivolity. They are allied, in Dumitru Tsepeneag's angelic characters, with a "haughty attitude, a provocative mien," which Baudelaire recognized in the dandy. Sad and withdrawn in his despairing pride more than serene and altruistic, the angel-dandy displays either an ironic smile, as in the short story "The Weeping," or a suave melancholy, as in "Homesickness." In both cases, the dandyism bears a Baudelairean resemblance to the stoical heroism of the eternal poseur, the one who aesthetically transfigures his suffering. "Homesickness" in particular is not only a text symptomatic of the special state of angelicality shared by Dumitru Tsepeneag's characters, but also a virtuoso inter-textual piece. To be more exact, we are dealing with an artistic palimpsest. The text allows us to glimpse, between the lines, the primary "text"—a painting by Magritte—reproduced on the cover of the first edition of the volume *The Wait*, published in 1972. Ultimately, Tsepeneag is creatively commenting on the painting of the surrealist artist, which depicts an enigmatic man-angel (the tails of his overcoat might also be angelic wings), guarded by a lion. Like the eagle in "Waiting," the lion is another incarnation of the protean angel, appearing in "The Weeping" and then in "The Accident" (where a flying enthusiast called old man Lion finds an injured angel), or in the short story "Prin gaura cheii" ["Through the Keyhole"], where the griffins or flying lions are oneiric/pathological representations of the protagonist. Tsepeneag's choice of Magritte is not without traces at the level of his prose, which can be felt, through an affinity of structure, in the figurative academicism and even in a certain programmatic primitivism on the part of the Belgian painter. On the other hand, the writer has in common with Dalí oneiric images drawn with paradoxical precision, like a photograph, also sharing, I think, the latter's tendency toward lithochronism, i.e. the reconversion of temporal sequences into a *simultaneous*[59] artistic vision.

To return to the angel as dandy, a central figure in the prose of Dumitru Tsepeneag, this seems to be in keeping with the vision as a whole of an alienated universe, in which, as in the absurd fable "Scaunele" ["The Chairs"] in the volume *Cold*, all that can be glimpsed from the top of the pyramid of chairs is nothingness instead of transcendence. A forgetful angel—he forgets his angelic function proper—or a dandy with egotistical inclinations, the protagonists of these stories are, in turn, the cause and the effect of universal desacralization. The protagonist nevertheless some-

59 Analyzing Tsepeneag's intention to make a "successive" art (Lessing) simultaneous, Romanian critic Ovidiu Moceanu notes: "The oneiric movement might be compared with an orientation in the modern world toward the visual, in concordance with the auditive, especially after the discovery of photography and film. The modern world's hunger for images explodes the interest in narrative." Ovidiu Moceanu, *Visul și literatura* [*The Dream and Literature*], 2 ed. (Pitești: Editura Paralela 45, 2002), 186.

times seems to accept, albeit only partly, his mystical condition. In the short story "The Weeping," for example, excessive weeping, with its expressionist hue, becomes an everyday attitude of the angel-dandy. Metamorphosed into Christ, he takes upon himself the sins of humanity and lets himself be crucified to the accompaniment of sadistic gales of laughter. The scene is grotesque and oneiric, sprinkled with nuances à la Urmuz or Daniil Kharms: ". . . and they come to poke the body crucified on the tree with everything they have: hairpins, tin tacks, paperclips, ballpoint pens, a razor, and even a small fork, of the kind for traveling. An old woman approaches timidly, she takes from her old, shabby handbag some knitting needles, and pokes them into his belly. He no longer laughs, he merely smiles approvingly or even encouragingly." The strange bird with yellow, glassy eyes in the short story "The Bird" is also an angel, a harbinger of death, a death which here has erotic connotations. No different is the case of "The Wait," which apothe-otically closes the collection of the same title. The novella is taken as a pretext by the author in *Novel for Reading on the Train*, which transposes the story of the making of a film based on it. Also by an accident of fate (as in "The Accident"), a *strange* woman of unreal beauty arrives at the railway station, bringing with her an eagle in a birdcage. An angel of death, the eagle is allowed to grow freely in the forest. Preparing for its return as though for a final, supreme effort, the railroad man shaves daily, dresses in new clothes, and scans the sky "with eyes moist with joy."

By his ecstatic *wait*, a kind of hermetic prayer, the human being is restored, in the work of Dumitru Tsepeneag, his own angel, also regaining, even if only in (aesthetic) dream or in death, his potential for the absolute. In other words, the oneiric/fictional world, with its specific, trans-subjective (angelic) imagery ultimately affirms not only the eternal aporia of its own condition, but also its own *mysticism*.

Țepeneag, Tsepeneag, Pastenague—the fictionalization of a hybrid identity • The theatricality of author/character viewpoint • The musicality of narrative structure • The surrealist-painting simultaneity of oneiric prose • The event/meaning born at the boundary of fiction

Dumitru Țepeneag's Parisian double can be found, more often than not, under the exotic—for the French—signature D. Tsepeneag. Or, as in the case of the novel *Pigeon vole* or the translation of Alexandre Kojève's book about Hegel, under that of Ed Pastenague. The anagram seems to have the role of marking an increasingly accentuated fictionalization of the in any case hybrid identity of the Franco-Romanian writer. What becomes visible is a tense oscillation between two linguistic and cultural identities, between two or more authorial periods, or even between two novelistic continents—Europe, East and West, and America, as in the trilogy of apparently realist novels made up of *Hotel Europa*,[60]

60 Bucharest: Editura Albatros, 1996; the French version, translated byAlain Paruit, was published in the same year in Paris, by Éditions P.O.L; the German version, translated by Ernest Wichner, was published in Berlin, by Alexander Fest Verlag, in 1998; Wichner, Frankfurt am Main, Suhrkamp Verlag, 2000 (Taschenbuch); the novel has also been translated into Hungarian and

Pont des Arts,[61] and *Maramureş*.[62] It tends to resolve itself, but in a Sisyphean way, in the "fugue" along the ambiguous boundary between fiction and reality. Symptomatic of the brisk zigzag movement of Dumitru Tsepeneag's fictive silhouettes, directed by the author supra-character and seconded by the reader infra-character, is a title such as *Zadarnică e arta fugii* [*Vain Art of the Fugue*].[63] Emancipated from under the tutelage of the Author, in the spirit of Pirandello, as early as the textualist script "Înscenare"

Slovenian (2002) and Czech (2008). The English version, with the title *Hotel Europa*, was published, in a translation by Patrick Camiller, by Dalkey Archive Press in 2010.

61 Bucharest: Editura Albatros, 1999; the French version, translated by Alain Paruit, was published in 1998 by Éditions P.O.L.

62 Cluj: Editura Dacia, 2001; with the title *Au pays du Maramureş*, translated by Alain Paruit, it was published in the same year by Éditions P.O.L; it was republished in 2006 by Editura Corint, Bucharest.

63 With the same title, it was published two decades later, by Editura Albatros (Bucharest, 1991), winning the writer the Prize of the Romanian Writers Union. The French version, entitled *Arpièges*, was published by Flammarion in 1973, translated by Alain Paruit. It was the writer's first novel signed under the name Dumitru Tsepeneag to be published in France. Dating from 1969–1971, *Arpièges* was launched in France at the peak of the nouveau roman period. According to Nicolae Bârna (see his monograph, *Ţepeneag. Introducere întro lume de hîrtie* {*Tsepeneag: Introduction to a World of Paper*}, [Bucharest: Editura Albatros, 1998], 145), related books are *La Bataille de Pharsale* (a novel that invokes Zeno and has as its hyper-text the aporia of Achilles and the tortoise) and *Triptique* by Claude Simon, and also *Projet pour une révolution à New York*, by Alain Robbe-Grillet. Proof of the critical success enjoyed by *Arpièges* in Paris is the review of the book by Jean Ricardou, the theoretician of the nouveau roman ("Les recherches de Tsepeneag," in *Le Monde*, no. 8922, 20 September 1973, 25), and also the fact that Tsepeneag's name was put forward for the Médicis Prize (won in the end by Milan Kundera), the most prestigious prize for foreign writers; see also Claude Bonnefoy, "Un mécanisme savant," in *La Quinzaine Littéraire*, no. 159, 1973, 14–15; Ilina Gregori, "Aspects de l'onirique dans la prose de Dumitru Tsepeneag," in *Cahiers de l'Est*, no. 20, 1980, 109–122. In 2007, the novel was published by Dalkey Archive Press in the United States, with the title *Vain Art of the Fugue*, translated into English by Patrick Camiller.

[A Staging], Dumitru Tsepeneag's characters opt either for self-immolation and self-immobilization in archetypal oneiric *images*, or for the dissolution of their increasingly evanescent identities in unruly picaresque ambulation. It is amplified, for example in *Hotel Europa* or in *Maramureş*, by the textual vertigo that moves from the interior towards the exterior of the novelistic universe, from the frame to the fiction, and vice versa.

Hence the programmatically "spiraling" movement of Tsepeneag's prose, which is otherwise also due to the effect of "petrified vertigo" in the French nouveau roman. A translator of some of the nouveaux romanciers, the (proto-)textualist and oneiric Romanian writer in his turn cultivates the method of the vain art of the petrified fugue. In other words, the Eleatic paradox of the motionless arrow, here transposed at a discursive level. Like nouveau romancier Claude Simon, Tsepeneag even resorts to an inter-textual adaptation of Zeno's paradox (an athlete, Pamfile, in *Vain Art of the Fugue*, manages to catch up with a tortoise while it is "asleep"). As early as the short stories of his youth (veritable paintings, in which words become patches of color, as in "Engraving," "Gurru" and "Homesickness"), but no less in his recent novels set in post-Revolution Romania, the writer prefers the exceptional fascination that can be aroused in the reader/viewer by the image in relation to the irremediably degraded word. (In *Maramureş*, there are frequent distortions of verbal language: for example, in the era of globalization, a stilted "Franco-Hungarian" or "Anglo-Hungarian" is spoken in Budapest.)

In the scenario or poem-essay "Pe pragul paradisului" ["On the Threshold of Paradise"], in the collection of short stories *Through the Keyhole*,[64] "words are nothing more than thumbtacks," while non-verbal language, or to be more precise the image, sheds a blinding, paradisiacal light, that of a "divine eye fixed upon me for an instant." It thus acquires, by the very immobilization of perception in such an "eternal" instant, a redemptive meaning. The paradisiacal "eternity" of the image in relation to the substitutive nature of the word, that of an ontological supplement (as for Derrida), is ensured by the presence of a number of compulsive phantasms. The return of the repressed, generative of catharsis, unfolds through a spiraling movement of the text-world (or, to use a phrase from *Pigeon vole*, according to an "echo structure"). In *Pigeon Post*, the writer explicitly refers to the technique of the spiral narrative, whereby the text gives the impression of continuing ad infinitum: "My spiral might stop and then continue . . . It is a simultaneously open and closed structure . . . I am inspired by music, dear sir. But it is not a matter of simple thematic modification . . . or of facile leitmotif . . . it is rather a matter of ghosts, thematic ghosts, do you understand? Entities that return . . . ectoplasms, things or beings, what does it matter? To come back, as you can see, their color is a little different . . . the same as their meaning . . ."

The sentences of Ed Pastenague bring to mind Saul Steinberg's 1964 meta-drawing, entitled *Spiral*, which might function as a hermeneutic key, as a revelatory mise en abyme for the entire work (specular par excellence) of Dumitru Tsepeneag. At the center of Steinberg's spiral can be found the one who is drawing, and the outer ring contains a sketch of a rural landscape (a few

64 *Prin gaura cheii* [*Through the Keyhole*], with a preface and notes by Nicolae Bârna (Bucharest: Editura Allfa, 2001).

trees, a wisp of cloud, a cottage on a hill). The man (the Creator) dominates the landscape, as a kind of god that lingers, with serene indifference, in the celestial space above his own creation. Consequently, everything (including himself) is his creation, and the signature and not least the title of the composition belong to him. Such a "reading" of the spiral signed by Saul Steinberg considers the drawing to be a fiction self-generated through continuous re-representation of self. As an "effigy" that contains its own spatial dynamism, it corresponds, I think, to the interpretation that Tsepeneag, as the main theoretician (and practitioner), alongside Leonid Dimov, of the aesthetic or structural Oneiricism of the 1960s; it lends itself to the text as an autotelic, non-referential "reality": "Like the dream, the oneiric text does not necessarily relate to a reality prior to the text." Invoking the concept of "restricted inter-textuality," of which Jean Ricardou, the theoretician of the nouveau roman and *Tel-Quel*-ism, spoke, Tsepeneag sees his work as a deliberately spiraling process of textual production, which is to say, one achieved through "the uninterrupted expansion of a number of themes, motifs or image nuclei, which cross from one text into another."

There are numerous literary "ectoplasms," in fact mises en abyme of imagery that *open up* the text of Tsepeneag's short stories and novels, as so many vanishing points for the moment of final revelation: the hunter without a rifle, the eagle with outstretched wings, the fish in flight, the acrobats caught up in the heat of performance, the girl with a skipping rope, the flocks of sheep sliding downhill, the flying saucers or airplanes with seemingly zoomorphic features, the wolf-woman or the goat-woman, but also the maternal ingénue figure of Mary in the *à rebours* Christ-like scene entitled "Staging," the metaphysical *wait* and the gaze that attempts to go *beyond*, into unreality, passing through an enchanted eyeglass or "through the keyhole," the angel wings of apparently profane creatures (the numerous angelic and at the same time grotesque wings in the short stories and novellas and, more recently, the cherub postman in *Hotel Europa*), the living wound or the living, moving spot, that mysteriously appears on the wall as a sign of an occult force (in the 1961 short story "The Specialist," but also in the novels *The Necessary Marriage* and *Maramureş*). The writer's ambition to adapt these thematic phantoms seems, as he himself admits, to be one that is musical. But it is also, as we shall see, pictorial or theatrical to an equal degree.

*

In *Maramureş*, a certain Silbermann advises the narrator-character: "If literature doesn't work any more, try painting." As early as the programmatic *Şotron* [*Hopscotch*] entitled, following Lessing, "Ut pictura poesis," Tsepeneag designated painterliness and pregnant visuality as defining features of the oneiric aesthetic. Likewise, he considered that Emil Brumaru, Daniel Turcea, and Leonid Dimov "*write* paintings." Theorizing the Oneiricism of the 1960s and '70s, Dumitru Tsepeneag draws from the dream the laws for construction of the imaginary and tends to transfer the oneiric dialectic to the structure of the text, in order to achieve "a kind of painted music, a music of time endlessly converted into space" ("The Oneiric Endeavor, after the War"[65]). The theoretical aim is to activate a complementariness between the poetics of André

65 *Momentul oniric*, 219.

Breton and Paul Valéry, which had been unsuspected and latent up until the oneiricists. And the descendents of Valéry, among whom Dumitru Tsepeneag counts himself, with justified pride in his own theoretical option, had the revelation of the production of the text from within itself, without relating to any pre-existing referent. It was thus Tsepeneag who discovered textualism as a result of the amendments he regarded as being required by the idea of automatic writing. Discovering the authentic novelty of Surrealism in the idea of simultaneity, Tsepeneag argues for an organic transition of surrealist writing into textualist construction: "Automatic writing as a literary method was doomed to failure: no one uses it as such any more. But this failure bore fruit, because it facilitated the appearance of a subtler notion: that of producing the text by means of the text itself. Thanks to automatic writing, the principle of an anterior reality, of an action necessarily preexistent to writing, could be contradicted in our times by the theoretical successors of Valéry. For them, the author is no longer the possessor of an established meaning, but merely a scriptor, the product of his own product. And the text is a medium for transformation, a privileged locus of metamorphoses."[66] Before analyzing the hypostases of the discursive role of the author *written* by his own text in the short prose and novels of Tsepeneag, however, I shall return to the hybrid literary genre of the oneiric texts.

As a serial art, like music, literature therefore also adopts the simultaneity specific to painting, which, according to the oneiricists, is to be found above all in the surrealist paintings of de Chirico, Magritte, and Tanguy. Tsepeneag's aesthetic program for

66 Ibid.

the attainment of a spatiotemporal continuum, in which the serial perception of images would become *simultaneous*, as in de Chirico, Magritte, Dalí, Delvaux, and others, seems to me to have been confirmed, in its intention to transgress the boundaries between the arts, by the opinion of French theorist Antoine Compagnon, to which it forms a counterpoint. Compagnon, as if providing a mirror image of Tsepeneag's thesis on the painterliness of the text, argues for the "literary" character of the Surrealists' plastic representations: "Leur peinture est littéraire: telle est d'emblée la limite de son expérimentalisme. Elle persiste à privilégier la représentation, fût-elle celle de fantasmes, au lieu d'explorer les possibilités du médium. La preuve en est dans l'importance du titre, et du jeu du texte et de l'image, qui devient rapidement une composante majeure de la peinture dite surréaliste."[67]

But the aspiration to attain this "painted music," associated with a phantasmic "time" endlessly convertible into space, also reveals itself, thanks to its trans-disciplinary syncretism, as well as the dynamism intrinsic to such a perspective on the creative act, to be one that is profoundly theatrical. It concentrates on the *rhythm* and the performative unfolding of the narrative act before a supposedly complicit reading audience, situated inside the textual frame (or an audience viewed in its turn by the textual "painting," the fiction, which gazes outside itself). In any case, in the first months of his Parisian exile, Tsepeneag had the revelation of the existence of an oneiric theater in the work of American director

67 Antoine Compagnon, *Les cinq paradoxes de la modernité* (Paris : Éditions du Seuil, 1990), 102–103. See also Antoine Compagnon, *The Five Paradoxes of Modernity*, trans. by Franklin Philip (New York: Columbia University Press, 1994).

Robert Wilson, whose performances he admiringly describes as being "of an exasperating slowness." Wilson is invoked once again in the novel *Maramureş*, in connection with the paradoxical mobile/immobile image of New Yorkers who practice jogging: "Men and women of all ages were running around the park, each at his own pace, each alone. Rarely, they combined in twos or threes. Because of the very different rhythms, it all looked like a performance staged by the famous Bob Wilson."

As in the case of Wilson's theatrical essays or happening-type performances, the moment of creation tends to be superposed over the moment of perception, and another passage from *Maramureş* is symptomatic in this sense: the seemingly petrified movement across the sky of derisory simulacra of transcendence reverberates, with a specularity typical of Tsepeneag's prose, in the sculpturally mobile image of the body of a young man running—a mise en abyme of the mechanism whereby the entire narrative is produced: "An airplane glides silently across the sky, resembling more a shark than an eagle or other animal endowed with wings. On the riverbank near the Academie, a still-youthful man is running. He seems interested in nothing other than his own running, in his body that is on the way to secreting its daily endorphin." At one point, the caustic Dr. Wolk makes fun of Dr. Gachet's intention to have his portrait painted: "I say he should paint you while jogging." Dr. Wolk's words allow the very method whereby the text is generated to be glimpsed, that of a moving meta-picture, as in Saul Steinberg, of the spiraling around an axis. On the other hand, Dr. Gachet's name contains another relevant intertextual reference: Gachet, in reality Van Gogh's physician, becomes the narrator's friend in *Hotel Europa*. It no longer appears at all surprising that the author meta-character chooses as a fictional projection painters or directors (the latter former painters, like Robert Wilson or Tadeusz Cantor), who, in their work, do not present a pre-existent text, but rather *write* mises-en-scènes or paintings, by means of the hieroglyphics specific to performance.

For example, a splendid painting, scripturally "painted" according to the principle of theatricality intrinsic to dream sequences, can be found in *Maramureş*, in the scene of the Metro train which passes through the (fictional, of course) station of Chèvres-Badelaine without stopping. After the already mentioned method of the moving spiral which, twisting around its own axis, institutes the novelistic world, the principles of ectoplasms and nuclei of numinous fascination, principles of oneiric imagery specific to Tsepeneag, are here activated. First of all, the viewpoint of the viewer (painter), of the authorial character, is one that is in motion. His vision will be increasingly anamorphosed by the "enormous sense" and "monstrous sight" presupposed by his capacity as lay magician of the performance after the eclipse: "I don't stop. I'm peddling furiously on a bicycle that they probably gave me at the entrance. On my head they placed a garnet-red hat in the form of a cone, a magician's hat." Into this Balkanic fairground atmosphere, which spontaneously updates Caragiale's "La Moşi," the mobile stage of the metro makes its entrance, but moving slowly, à la Wilson, and displaying to the "applauding" audience images of parodic surreality, of Artaud-like cruelty: "pink and purple cows," "the life-size portrait of Dimov," "piglets with the apple of knowledge in their snouts, Renaissance cardinals," "stenographers with venomous snakes at their bosom, a rapacious policeman." Then, similarly, "weather-cocks, termagants, a crucified conjurer," "Joan of Arc in a nightshirt visited by English bowmen," "Marie Antoinette with her head in her lap as Robespierre and Marat whisper in each other's ear and laugh as though at a good joke," "here too are Napoleon Bonaparte and Josephine in an intimate moment, from which it emerges that the emperor was rather poorly endowed by nature." Finally, "Hitler, Stalin and other stars of history," but also "Ceauşescu and his wife during their trial."

The viewpoint of the subject that *sees* and, by means of the demiurgic gaze, directs the novelistic play oscillates between distance from the inner spectator of its own epic performance and empathy toward its own characters. There exists here a structural duality, transcribed through the alternation of the apparent objectivity of the oneiric-textual "spectacle," fixed in the seemingly petrified pictoriality of the painting-scenes, on the one hand, and the dynamic of the kinetic spectacle, of the often Caragiale-like "carnival" of the text-images that unfold in film sequence.

One of the characters adopts, as was to be expected, the role of the most well-informed reader possible, i.e. the critic who also breaks the convention of the fourth wall and nonchalantly and assertively enters the inner stage of the novel. With slight literary distaste for "that incompetent, two-bit writer," he draws attention to the mythic-fictional nature of Maramureş, a region which "is not as he thinks or wants to think. Maramureş is his Yoknapatamangaphawa." And the imaginary Metro train that continuously passes through this *possible world* will probably be an oneiric Ouroboros, this time mechanical, or a snail (of meta-narrative) in its autotelic shell, a bicephalous creature belonging to the zone of both the fictional and the real. A double grotesque of the writer-director, originating from an ambiguous realm, with anthropomorphic, zoomorphic and mechanomorphic features, it retraces, in reverse, the trajectory of the painter as depicted by Saul Steinberg. Emerging from the flesh of the Author ("holy body and nourishment to itself"), the imaginary Metro train becomes pure, linear abstraction, and finally, when the spiral closes, it becomes nature once more, a landscape created by the true, demiurgic, celestial Scriptor.

*

The narrator's narcissistic image of his own corporeality (or of the corporeality of the woman, Marianne, who shrinks only to expand once more, like Alice in Wonderland) yet again provides a fictional effigy of the process of textual expansion and contraction. The subject/corporeality/text relationship is symbiotic. The dissemination of the subject results in the intertextuality and discursivity of the novel, and vice versa, the transgressive writing in its turn has repercussions on the increasingly fluctuating identity of the "textuator." An adept of Pirandello-like humor, the author-character of *Pont des Arts* proposes to "look in the mirror as I write." Thanks to this specular posture, he achieves a distanced state, an anti-Einfühlung, becoming in the moment of self-mirroring a spectator-character on the epic "stage," who himself remains on the stage when the others, the fictional characters properly speaking, "recite" their lines. The narrator too looks in the mirror at the beginning of the first novel in the trilogy, *Hotel Europa*, as well as in the final, terminal novel of the narrative cycle, *Maramureş*, emblematically rediscovering himself in the fetal position, curled up in his own corporeal and at the same time textual shell. But the first-person of *Hotel Europa* ("I unstick my knee from her thigh, let out a faint groan as I turn over") becomes, at the end of *Maramureş* a third-person ("the man alongside lifts his knee from his thigh, groaning softly"), in the logic the evolution towards an increasingly accentuated novelistic objectification of scriptural narcissism. The *I* that has become a *he* does not, however, transform itself into an object, into a *that*, but rather it is also a fictionalized *fellow man* (in the terms of Levinas). What is thereby achieved is the plenitude of the spiral, of the fictionally integrated biography, of the fiction always open to the biographical, of the painting looking outside of its frame. In the words of Gide, in *Paludes*, it might be said that what appears here is the story of the third person, which is spoken, which exists in each of us and does not die with us.

The apotheotic finale of the trilogy brings with it "the combination of the venerable—revitalized—myths of Mioriţa and the Grail with the modern (trivialized, popularized, commercialized) millenarian myth of extraterrestrials,"[68] with the author being extracted, separated from the immanence of his own language by an occult force, in any case one that transcends

68 Nicolae Bârna, "Yoknopatamangaphawa, liniştea sufletului şi 'finalul deschis' etern" [Yoknopatamangaphawa, tranquillity of the soul and the eternal 'open ending'], in *Apostrof*, no. 12, 2001, 4; Nicolae Bârna, *Prozastice* [*Prosaistics*], (Bucharest: Editura Institutului Cultural Român, 2004), 107.

the text (signaled by the parodic/numinous appearance of a UFO, whose steps he climbs, the same as in the cosmic marriage to the "flaming stars" in Miorița). The taste for the postmodern sensationalism of cinematic fiction, often of a hyperrealist, thriller or sci-fi kind, reaffirms an aesthetic of the surface, one that is always specific in the wake of the nouveau roman, to the prose of Dumitru Tsepeneag. The detective novel "façade" or screen in *Maramureș* (the novel within the novel, whose protagonists are the invalid Gică and his girlfriend, Amina, in search of a Fra Angelico miniature) is a reflection of the author's preoccupation with semantic *surfaces*, transposed into images in all their quasi-oneiric transparency. Referring to the conceptual metaphor of the *mirror* in the works of Lewis Carroll, Gilles Deleuze defined the logic of meaning in phrases that might be compared precisely with Tsepeneag's paradoxical Oneiricism, i.e. with the writer who organizes and stylistically constricts his text (thus reminding us of the members of the Oulipo group) with the lucidity of an inveterate chess player. This is because the meaning of the texts written by Tsepeneag, a "post-Valéryian"[69] author, arises at the boundary of biographical fiction, "on the curb of the sidewalk" (to use a phrase from the title of a short story in the volume *Cold*).

Meaning *appears*, as Deleuze would say, at the *surface*, in that fine, incorporeal mist that detaches itself from bodies, an enveloping pellicle, without volume, a mirror that reflects them.[70]

69 Ion Vartic, "Din mansarda dlui Teste pe targa lui Gracchus" [Out of the Mansard of Mr. Teste on the Stretcher of Gracchus], in *Apostrof*, no. 5, 2001, 4; see also Ion Vartic, *Pont des Arts*, in *Dicționar analitic de opere literare românești* [*Analytical Dictionary of Romanian Literary Works*], definitive edition, ed. Ion Pop, vol. II, N-Z (Cluj: Casa Cărții de Știință, 2007), 824.

70 See Gilles Deleuze, *Logique du sens*, (Paris, Minuit, 1969), 19–20.

Like Alice through the looking glass, Marianne, the feminine alter ego of the narrator in the *Hotel Europa–Pont des Arts–Maramureş* trilogy, liberates her incorporeal double. Of a rare vigor in its epic development and the structure of its imagery, Dumitru Tsepeneag's trilogy makes sense at the edges of the narrative spiral or at the surface of the fictional pellicle. The metaphysics of the traditional novel is now transformed into a self-mirroring hermeneutics of self, of a novelist-character, who looks beyond himself, "through the keyhole," as though through a fascinating reverse looking glass, into the world of the *third person.*

THE IMAGOLOGICAL DECONSTRUCTION OF THE CHARACTER

The third-person novel and partial objectivization of narrative viewpoint • The demythologization of Romanianism • *La belle Roumaine* and the alterity of the identity of Ana/Hannah: the condition of the feminine, Jewishness, and being Eastern in an ex-communist country • The parodic novel and the roman à clef • The clichés of imagology regarding Romanianism • Anti-psychologism and the hybrid subject

An internal necessity in the evolution of Dumitru Tsepeneag's prose since the year 2000 seems to have been the objectivization of discourse and the attainment of additional novelistic verisimilitude. This is organically linked to an increasingly evident thematic choice: *Romanianism*, explored not only in fiction proper, but also in the essay (in *Reîntoarcerea fiului la sînul mamei rătăcite* [*The Son's Return to the Bosom of the Errant Mother*] and *Destin cu Popeşti* [*A Destiny with the Priestly*]. The Franco-Romanian's most recent novel, *La belle Roumaine*,[71] continues to mythologize the phantasm of his native land, although in the imagological perspective[72] there can be felt a negative, self-flagellating patriotism, reminiscent of that displayed by Emil Cioran in *Schimbarea la față a României* [*The Transfiguration of Romania*].

The mythologization of the image of Romania contains a parody of itself, given the post-Brechtian distance of the narrator character, as well as his distance from himself and from any eventual sentimental "trap" of empathizing with the reader. What takes place here is a mise en abyme of the imagological cliché regarding the beauty (geographical, "spiritual," etc.) of the native land and its hospitality, translated by its parodic reversal, of complete erotic availability towards foreigners. Ana, alias Hannah, is the femme fatale capable, thanks to her insatiable sensuality, of both perpetual erotic seduction and cynical detachment toward the trauma of her male victims. To be more precise, the trauma of her lovers, including the rudimentary and jealous Russian Yegor, the two sophisticated German philosophy teachers, Dieter and Johannes, the contemplative and hedonistic Turk Mehmet, and the suave barman Jean-Jacques, the only one who possesses the "beautiful Romanian woman" solely in his imagination.

---

71 Pitești: Editura Paralela 45, 2004; the French edition was published by P.O.L in 2006, trans. Alain Paruit; a new edition was published in 2007 by Editura Art, Bucharest.

72 An interdisciplinary field, at the confluence of ethno-psychology, the history of mentalities, politology, sociology, the history of the imaginary, and comparative literature, imagology—the term coined by Daniel-Henri Pageaux—presupposes a methodology of comparative research into the stereotypical image of the alien, of collective mental constructs of alterity. At the same time, imagological studies analyze the way in which an ethnic, national community or even trans-national cultural units (Francophony, Pan-Germanism, Pan-Slavism) process and interiorize mental clichés of the identity of the Other.

A quasi-ironic novel and/or roman à clef, *La belle Roumaine* wagers on the detective-like complicity of the reader, to whom it provides an opportunity for intellectual jubilation at calculating the alternation of revelation/concealment in the parabolic meaning. The much craved *truth* regarding the always ambiguous identity of the protagonist or that regarding the circumstances of her murder, as well as the author(s) of the crime, remain mysteries that remain un-deciphered until the end of the novel—an open ending, thanks to the conflicting tension that is perpetuated even by the suspense of the last sentence. Structured polyphonically, according to the laws of the fugue and counterpoint, the entire text (and along with it the specular, textually mirroring figure of Ana, "la belle Roumaine") highlight not so much a certain *meaning* as much as a non-figurative semantics or a *non-semantic* that is specifically musical. A poetic art of the novel (which translates, as a whole, the symptomatic dissemination of the female character metonymically) can also be read in the suggestions that Ana is given by her Romanian lover, Securitate officer Mihai, the "director" in the shadows, the one who had initiated her in her international espionage career, first in the German Democratic Republic, then, after 1989, in France: "'You should always keep up an artistic flow,' he said, laughing. 'Let the interlocutors fill in the blank spaces . . . Don't be afraid of pauses. That's their role. Like in poetry!'" On the other hand, not following his advice to the letter, Ana pursues her own bovarist urges, unfolding for lovers of various nationalities "concocted stories, but not entirely so, merely half-concocted ones, for that was her technique: she would set out from a real fact and embroider around it. The real fact . . . would thus be so life-like that it projected veracity onto the rest as well," so that "when she told a story, she herself believed what she was telling." Whereas to the Russian Yegor she presents herself as a Romanian originally from the Maramureş region, whose father had been a prisoner in the Stalinist Gulag, for the two German philosophers, Dieter and Johannes, Ana becomes a resentful Jewess, Hannah Silbermann. In conformity with an oneiric pseudo-logic or by means of a mythomaniacal self-delusion, she insists on inducing feelings of guilt, invoking the atrocious fate of her parents, prisoners in Auschwitz. This cliché of imagology, treated in the novel with subtle parody, does not, however, exclude subjacent empathy with the character's tribulations, who seems to attribute to herself, more phantasmically than not, a Jewish identity.

The Don-Juanism of Ana's (Hannah's) relationship with her own always fluid and self-deconstructed identity is primarily visible in the intrinsic theatricality of the Don Juan myth. The protagonist successively changes masks or the projective roles of the "I," resembling now Elvire Popesco, the celebrated actress of Romanian origin, now a common or garden prostitute from the Bois de Boulogne. Then, the "musical" spontaneity of her eroticism is equivalent to the "sensual genius" (the sine qua non component of the myth, remarked upon as such by Kierkegaard about Mozart's *Don Giovanni*) with which she fascinates her skeptical European erotic and political partners. The same as the archetypal Don Juan, the protagonist is pure erotic, political and, in general, existential *availability*, or, to paraphrase Camus' verdict on the inherent absurdity of Don-Juanism, she "has chosen to be nothing." Like the fatal Lulu, Wedekind's protagonist (and later that of Alban Berg), Ana puts up resistance against any attempt to be depicted, and thus completely possessed, objectified: "Perhaps quite simply the abstract motifs of the shirt, of the blouse, constitute the genuine subject of the painting." Her sooner generic, unspecific figure—a rather "commercial" blonde, reminiscent of an "American actress freshly arrived from Hollywood"—evokes nothing more than an impersonal photo-fit portrait, of the kind used in criminal investigations. The rejection of the figurative ultimately signifies the refusal of Ana's partners to recognize her in the alterity of her irreducible subjectivity, but also her refusal fully to offer herself to them, to let herself be manipulated by the reductive desires of the male subjects.

The place of punitive transcendence, of the Commander in Don Juan, or of deus ex machina ethical censorship in Wedekind's drama (embodied in the literary figure of Jack the Ripper, who murders Lulu), is this time provided by an enigmatic and anxious *empty subject*. The murderer, thus the unseen director (probably, within a textualist interpretation, the author-character himself), remains unidentified. He may be her much invoked conational Mihai, or one of her many European or American partners, or even the oneiric/thanatic eagle in the cage (a figuration of Ana's *animus*?), which sometimes metamorphoses, in the fictional dream, into a parrot with red, yellow and blue feathers, the colors of the Romanian flag . . . Nor is the subtextual suggestion of an act of suicide lacking. Ana's Don-Juanism metaphorically translates as a stereotype of *Romanianism*, namely excessive hospitality and diplomacy, in themselves somehow suicidal.

Beyond the passionate philosophical debates, the anthropological essays and the comparative imagology, organically included in the mix of the novel, the ineffable Don-Juanesque existence of the beautiful Romanian woman—a mythologized and sooner non-referential character, often a purely textual reflection—may, on the other hand, be accessible to a primarily "musical" approach. It is this that Dumitru Tsepeneag's novel, meticulously cast according to the principle of narrative polyphony, sets out to achieve—and does so successfully.

*

In the same lineage as his favorite writer, Franz Kafka, and in consonance with the poetics of the nouveau roman, Dumitru Tsepeneag programmatically rejects the formula of psychological prose, regarding it, presumably, as out of date, fastidious and even pedantic, aesthetically speaking. The explanation can be found in a revealing sentence in *Hotel Europa*, in which the narrator deplores the tautological and inevitably clichéd nature of inner language about ourselves. The inflation of psychologizing discourse is supposed to originate from the eternal, Sisyphean going around in circles of any introspective self-analysis.[73] Wearily contemplating in the mirror his indubitable signs of aging, the character always recognizes *another*, undertaking with apparent detachment a kind of course of self-analysis in front of a probably condescending *double*, or an imaginary, presumably ironic audience:

73 The deviation of Tsepeneag's novels from the post-Proustian psychological technique resides, according to Eugen Simion, in the fact that "the flow relates sooner to the epic discourse, and less, if at all, to the inner life of the characters" (see "Personajele realiste în căutarea autorului oniric" [Realist Characters in Search of an Author], in *Cultura*, no. 22, 18 May 2006, 9).

> I stand up, go to the bathroom, and switch on the light. I experience it as an assault. Raise my arm to parry the blow.
>
> Then I see myself in the mirror.
>
> We always think about ourselves in clichés: the same words keep seeping into our consciousness, forming a kind of schematic, coded monologue that at least has the merit of preserving some mental continuity. On the other hand, what's the point of repeating over and over again something that can no longer be called an observation, still less an appraisal of a particular state of affairs, because it's no longer linked to reality directly through a process of perception, but only vaguely through one of recognition—not an image but an idea, and in the end an *idée fixe*? I don't take the trouble to verify it: I've grown old!

The onerous cobbling together of an identity occurs, from the very beginning of the novel, within a predominantly compartmentalized perspective. The "I" slowly comes to its senses in the fetal position. Then it barely registers, as if from outside itself, with a certain affective neutrality, the clash with the objects of the external world. The apparently disembodied gaze, detached from its bearer, settles on them one by one:

> I unstick my knee from her thigh, let out a faint groan as I turn over thinking of the word sciatica. Then my hand knocks against the wood of the bedside table—an agreeable sensation. I ought to be getting up.

> It's pitch-dark in the room, winter outside. I can only just make out the tree branches at the window: threatening or protective, I'm not sure which. A huge skeleton preserved in the cold.

Occasionally reinvigorated by a fleeting "agreeable sensation," the mind, it too reified, around an *idée fixe*, utters *aging*. It might all too well belong not only to the alienated cognizant human subject, but also, in the tradition of "objectualist" prose, precisely to the specular object, to the mirror: "I've grown old! Is this a leitmotif of mine, or the mirror's?"

The scene with the mirror, with the entire ritual concomitant upon daily self-contemplation in *Hotel Europa*, signals from the start Tsepeneag's option, synonymous with that expressed by the narrator within the text, for a cinematic, anti-psychologizing prose. The alienated and mechanized thought—in this case, that of rapidly advancing old age—of the character seems to the character himself more like a "label" or the "subtitles for a silent film," voided of subjective content:

> It's no longer a question of angst; it's become something mechanical by dint of repetition, like the flicking of a switch. It's not a thought but a label stuck to the mirror, an intertitle in a silent movie. Or a subtitle in a sound movie in a different language: I see an image with the word underneath; I no longer try to fight it, as I would have done a few years ago, nor to study it more attentively, to inspect it for plausible arguments against this "accusation," to plead that at least there are extenuating circum-

> stances. I no longer defend myself in any way. I shrug my shoulders—and the accusation becomes a verdict, a final sentence.
>
> Without thinking I grab the toothbrush and toothpaste. I always squeeze out too much. I turn on the tap . . .

An almost robotized character, worn out by the impotence of old age, by sciatica and by the insane jealousy of his wife, as well as by writer's block, the novelist of *Hotel Europa* teleports himself by way of compensation into the space of his own novelistic fiction. In other words, he enters through a portal into the world behind the mirror, as a grotesquely parodic and world-weary reflection of Lewis Carroll's ingenuous main character. The scene where various fictional worlds are alternately perceived—that dominated by the huffy, nagging wife, Marianne, who bursts into the bathroom, on the one hand, and that littered with the protagonists (Mihai, Ion) the narrator-character is mentally writing, on the other—is an anthology piece:

> "Open the door! I need to brush my teeth." . . .
>
> She goes to the sink and turns the taps on, hard. Grabs her toothbrush with one hand, the tube of paste with the other. I admire the way her hips shake in time with her brush strokes. Vibrating all over, she tries to tell me something, an idea that develops in her as more and more of the toothpaste turns into froth. An idea or maybe an urgent message. I don't understand a word, but I do see that the mirror is becoming dotted with little white specks. I lie down again in the bath and remember that I can't

> leave Mihai rooted to the spot in the middle of the sidewalk, jostled on all sides by the people heading for the square. Probably he's already reached the meeting place and noticed that Ion isn't waiting there, that he's left—or never arrived.
>
> "—want a bath too!"
>
> The last few words were audible—and peremptory. No point in protesting, in saying that I wasn't finished, hadn't even had time to soap myself properly; nor in shamelessly divulging that because of her I had botched an important scene.

In Tsepeneag's novels, the frames of the various fictional and hybrid, referentially intermediate worlds are constantly being transgressed. Such a narrative structure recalls Peter Greenaway's film essay *Prospero's Books*, based on a script that rewrites Shakespeare's *The Tempest*. But, in Greenaway's pictorial/theatrical/cinematic discourse, the character of the creator (Prospero alias Shakespeare, alias God or merely a Gnostic demiurge) was dictatorial, whereas the author/narrator supra-character in the post-1989 novels of Tsepeneag is more often than not *vulnerable*. Or else he displays a circumspect and ingeniously mimicked vulnerability in front of his characters.

The "religion" of Dumitru Tsepeneag's narrator-character is a belonging to an ontological/aesthetic interstice, which also means a kind of *more-than-literature*. The "director" too has a narrative role that is now quasi-biographic, now quasi-fictional, zoomorphic, mechanomorphic, angelomorphic, or, quite simply, virtual.

This creator/creature, not being the Nietzschean Superman, is an authority only partly indebted to the idea of humanity, thus to affectivity and traditional rationality, and therefore only partly represented through anthropomorphic cryptograms. A *more-than-man* or *less-than-man*, which critically re-inscribes, within an oneiric, textualist, phantasmic, imagological, or biographical framework, a typological invariable, an archetype.

For, in the short prose and novels of Tsepeneag, the meta-literary passages are not legitimizing discourses, but rather *discourses of suspicion* toward the traditional, conventionally established aesthetic boundaries between various typologies of prose. Thus, between prose and, for example, narrative "pictopoetry,"[74] or between prose and the trans-textual, theatrical, scenographic, or cinematic scriptic discourse. Moreover, the meta-narrative sequences in the short stories and novels of Tsepeneag place under a question mark any belonging on the part of the characters to certain ontological categories. The boundaries between realms, regarded, in the quasi-oneiric possible world, as far too rigid, are also undermined. The result is that any separation of levels of fictionality from *levels of reality* (as Mario Vargas Llosa would say) becomes problematic.

74 To many prose texts by Tsepeneag, as well as epic-theatrical poems by Dimov, the term "picto-poetry," invented by Victor Brauner and Ilarie Voronca in the 1930s, might well be applied.

"Moftological" deconstruction of Romanianism • The inverse "Fiesco complex" • Cultural, linguistic and ethnic marginality/centrality • *Mioriticism*, oriental fatalism, self-castigation in the tradition of Caragiale and Cioran • *Maramureș* and the cosmic homeland • Patriotism/Europeanism and the hermeneutics of mythologized identity in *Les Noces nécessaires* • The *moft* of identity and the metaphysical *moft*

As early as in *Les Noces nécessaires*,[75] where the protagonist, Ciobanu, was the inverted, fictional/oneiric effigy of the shepherd in the ballad *Miorița*, Dumitru Tsepeneag begins to construct a paradoxical mythology of *Romanianism*. This will come to fulfillment in the trilogy of post-1989 Romania (*Hotel

75 The novel was first published in French, translated by Alain Paruit (Flammarion, 1977). The original Romanian version, entitled *Nunțile necesare*, was published by Editura Fundației Culturale Române (with serious printing errors), in 1992. A second edition, hors commerce, was published by Editura Ars Amatoria, also in 1992. In 1998, a third edition was published by Editura All, Bucharest.

Europa, Pont des Arts, Maramureş), the more recent pseudo-detective and imagological novel *La belle Roumaine*, as well as in a host of "şotroane" ["hopscotches"], polemical essays, cultural debates in the press, and interviews. The bilingual Franco-Romanian writer who defined himself as "exiled in exile" thereby accomplishes an expiatory and at the same time compensatory scriptural act. His stylistic and imaginary *homeland* is subject to successive parodic deconstruction and nonetheless skeptical reconstruction.

After giving up writing in his native tongue (the novel *Le Mot sablier / Cuvîntul nisiparniţă* [*The Sandglass Word*] is a *performance* text which transcribes precisely the drama of the transition from a Romanian to a French scriptural identity), by the time Dumitru Tsepeneag reaches the hyperrealistic novel *Hotel Europa* he already treats his dual Franco-Romanian identity with self-derision, with detached humor, but also with a kind of tender understanding. The very oscillation between two languages, between two cultures, between two categories of phantasms of identity, is a powerful generator of textual-imaginary constructs. In other words, between Ţepeneag and Tsepeneag, or, as author of the novel *Pigeon vole* and sometimes translator, Ed Pastenague. The following sentence might be invoked as a motto for his dual identity, that of a "Mioritic" given to self-derision and of a *uncountried* European: "Paraphrasing Herder, I like to say: 'My homeland is not a country, my homeland is the Romanian language.' So, for quite some time my exile was total, given that I had left not only the country but also the language. But now, returning to the language, returning now and again to the country, why is it that I do not feel I have wholly returned to the homeland?"[76]

Tsepeneag's paradoxical relationship with his status as a "Romanian in Paris" might, I think, be rethought by means of a comparison with the "moftological" deconstruction of Caragiale's image of the Romanian, but also with the self-castigating definitions of *Romanianism* made by famous exiles such as Emil Cioran (with his youthful anti-patriotic essays in *The Transfiguration of Romania*) and Eugène Ionesco (who, during his youth in Romania, exclaimed, self-deprecatingly: "If I had been French, I might have been a genius"). In connection with Ionesco and Cioran, but also with Caragiale, who toward the end of his life went into exile in Berlin, essayist Ion Vartic speaks of a *Fiesco complex*, as a trauma of major writers, "endowed with a hypertrophied individual consciousness, who feel suffocated in a small country . . . and in a minor culture, a 'poor relative' of the major cultures."[77] Even Hamlet suffered from the Fiesco complex, but the name Fiesco originates, in fact, in a play by Schiller, where Gian-Luigi Fiesco, named *il Giovane*, is "the impetuous archetype of the young genius who suffocates in the petty framework of a marginal space."[78] On the other hand, in theories of postmodern multiculturalism (Charles Taylor, Will Kymlicka, Seyla Benhabib, et al.), as well as in current cultural anthropology,

---

76 In *Războiul literaturii încă nu s-a încheiat. Interviuri* [*The Literature War is not Over. Interviews*], ed. Nicolae Bârna (Bucharest: Editura Allfa, 2000), 130.
77 Ion Vartic, *Clanul Caragiale* [*The Caragiale Clan*] (Cluj: Editura "Biblioteca Apostrof," 2002), 156.
78 Ion Vartic, *Cioran naiv și sentimental* [*Cioran Naïve and Sentimental*] (Cluj: Editura "Biblioteca Apostrof," 2000), 101.

such a discriminatory hierarchy, based on non-recognition and almost exclusion of *difference*, on the ostracism of the value of so-called *minor cultures*, has come to be considered unethical, and therefore unacceptable. Tsepeneag, in any case, being very up-to-date in his mindset as a *European* Romanian, does not entirely ascribe to it.

If we firstly take as a frame of reference for the condition of the Romanian exile the symptomatic *Fiesco complex*, the case of Dumitru Tsepeneag seems to me quite atypical and, for that reason, stimulating in its complexity. The writer's Romanian citizenship was revoked by Ceauşescu, by presidential decree, in 1975, and in 1978 his application for French citizenship was rejected. Therefore, as far as the forced exile of the 1960s theorist of aesthetic Oneiricism is concerned, it would be possible to argue for the existence of a Fiesco complex *à rebours*. Tsepeneag no longer relates to his Romanianism as primarily a trauma of identity, but more often in droll terms, with humor tinged with self-parodying bitterness, in the tradition of Caragiale. A humor that is aloof, ironical, "European." Tsepeneag adopts (ethnic, linguistic, cultural) marginality as a different kind of *centrality*: "The return to the Romanian language coincided with my physical (albeit temporary) return to the Romanian space, which had been barred to me for almost thirty years. Probably, in spite of the inherent disappointments parallel with the satisfactions, this too contributed to the reinvigoration of my writing. It pulled me out of an increasingly sterile formalism. It purified me. In short: it helped me to emerge from the ghetto. From marginalization. This is not a paradoxical formulation. For someone who writes in the Romanian language, the center is in Romania, not in Paris."[79] Much argued over today, the question of community identity is one that Tsepeneag tackles in a provocative, polemical way, in the tradition of Cioran's questions of what it means to be a Romanian. A "şotron" [hopscotch]—an invention of Tsepeneag's, a species of literary essay, often a form of squib, inheriting something of Caragiale's *moft* and *moment*—in *Destin cu Popeşti*[80] has as its title the very same despairing rhetorical question put by Cioran: *Comment peut-on être roumain?* Cioran's prophetic despair in *The Transfiguration of Romania* is interpreted in a nuanced way and compared with the *Mioriticism* theorized by Lucian Blaga, who was convinced that the national specific is conserved through isolation, through non-participation in history.

On the one hand, Tsepeneag rejects Mioriticism as fundamentally non-European, when it approaches oriental fatalism, nihilism and suicidal passivity. But he also re-mythologizes it in a surprising way, through the subtle hermeneutic he applies to the ballad that lies at the foundation of the myth. Although he argues that he does not believe in Mioriticism, or to be more precise in a "cultural morphology of the Blaga type," Tsepeneag justifies his appeal to the Mioritic myth in *Les Noces nécessaires/Nunţile necesare* [The Necessary Marriage] by the need to compensate for a biographical trauma within the imaginary space: the trauma of being driven from one's native land. But "from hence to the claim that Romanianism rests upon 'incurable vices' is a large step, one which I see no reason to take. Why do you think that

79 *Războiul literaturii . . .*, 218.

80 Cluj: Editura Dacia & Editura "Biblioteca Apostrof," 2001.

my pessimism has a local tinge?" Tsepeneag asks his interviewer, in a tone that is polemical and at the same time pedagogical. "If passivity, as you say, made it easier to impose Communism, in that case passivity ought to be a common trait of a number of very different nations. Take a little time to admire the ethnic diversity of the Socialist concentration camp!"[81] Referring in the same context to the characters of *Hotel Europa*—a motley assembly of swindlers, racketeers, prostitutes and gangsters, who are not only Romanians but also Russians, Arabs, Hungarians, Serbs, Germans, Greeks, and Japanese—the writer does not omit to specify that their "vices" are even more widespread than "the more or less ataractic passivity of the Mioritic shepherd." Moreover, the ballad *Miorița* would conceal, in the acceptance of death, a philosophy of life, as the revelation of death is, par excellence, humanized and at the same time generative of art. What is regarded as ataractic passivity in the Mioritic shepherd—or else as ahistorical abulia—is ultimately, as Tsepeneag argues, a state of artistic contemplation. In *Hotel Europa*, even the archetypal peasant, Ion, sometimes becomes an uncountried occasional philosopher, who haunts the urbane bohemia of Europe: "'Humor and transhumance—that's the genius of the Romanian people. We're all just comical nomads!' declared Ion, solemnly raising his brimming glass to his mouth and draining it in one gulp." Another sample of parodic imagology is the fictional re-inscription, in *Hotel Europa*, of a shocking news item reported in the Romanian press at the time. The story, also commented on in a 1997 issue of *Cahiers de l'Herne* dedicated to the Dracula myth,

81 Ibid., 269–270.

involved the rape, in a morgue, of the corpse of a woman, who is supposed to have then come back to life. Later, in *Maramureș*, the character Silbermann is impatient to visit, as a tourist, a Romania made famous thanks to the sensationalism of vampire films and to confirm his clichés about the land of Dracula: "Silbermann went on hoping that one fine day he would visit Dracula's castle. No one dared to tell him that Dracula's castle only existed in films and in the minds of Americans."

Separately from the imagery and textual core named *Hotel Europa*, the second novel in the trilogy, or even the projected epic tetralogy of post-1989 Romania, *Pont des Arts* brings back onto the stage discussions on themes of the politics and mindset of the characters, as well as their phantasms of identity. Caught up in a mad chase across Europe, one that is simultaneously narrative and phantasmic, they experience and conceptualize their Romanian-ness as a pre-written fatality, discovering themselves in the embroidery of a Caragialean palimpsest. Romanian identity is set up in effigy and then parodied by means of a rewrite of Caragiale's *Lost Letter*, within a new historical context of moral confusion and globalizing political projects. It is from here that inter-textual characters such as Fănică and Zoe Rotaru (this time man and wife, Zoe's lover being a communist, Hainăroşie [Redcoat], on the other hand). Remarking on the hallucinatory feeling produced in the reader by the unprecedented mixture of fiction, oneiric sequences and sensational, improbable newspaper items, Frédéric Joly finds in *Pont des Arts* "un texte diaboliquement brillant et dont l'humour et l'autodérision ne cherchent pas à masquer, bien au contraire, la condition fondamentalement solitaire de l'écrivain, immigré de toute société, et son absence d'illusions quant au futur d'une Europe délivrée de l'horreur totalitaire mais plongée dans un désenchantement lourd d'interrogations."[82] After *Pont des Arts* and the self-castigating vision of the Mioritic mentality in the context of a Europe itself adrift and emptied of traditional mythical points of reference, *Maramureş* reconstructs, through the prism of a seemingly affectionate parody, the Romanian mythology of Mioriticism. Maramureş, where the narrator-character will experience the cosmic wedding of the apotheotic finale of the novel, becomes, in counterpoint to Paris, New York, Vienna, Budapest, or Cluj, a *topos* of marginality transformed into a mythical-imaginary *center*. In this omphalos of the world, the rawness of origins encounters media sensationalism, touched by both kitsch and ahistorical poetry.

Here, too, Tsepeneag proves to be a late disciple of Caragiale's tender self-derision, aimed at the untranslatable Romanian *moft*. The Rebreanu-like character Ion of Glanetaş now becomes, in *Maramureş*, Ion of Planetaş. The *yearning* which, in Blaga's vision, dominates the Mioritic space, is replaced in the paradoxical and Caragialean novel of Tsepeneag with the *moft*, visible in the temporarily Europeanized and even globalized natives of Maramureş. Or in the vulgar and at the same time ineffable Ana (Hannah) of *La belle Roumaine*, whose erotic availability metaphorically betrays another stereotype of *Romanianism*: excessive hospitality and diplomacy, in themselves suicidal. The natives of Maramureş in the end return to their cosmic *homeland*. The

82 Frédéric Joly, "Les étranges grimaces de Dumitru Tsepeneag," in *Reg'Arts*, no 21, October 1998, 19.

impenetrable mystery of Ana's death—in which the oneiric eagle with the tricolor feathers presumably plays the same role as the Commander in *Don Juan*—mythologizes yet again the figure of the *beautiful Romanian woman*. The *moft* à la Dumitru Tsepeneag reveals its metaphysical dimensions, as well as those connected with identity.

III.

THE LONELINESS OF THE DEMIURGE
CONFRONTED WITH THE EMANCIPATION OF THE CHARACTER

The Pirandello-esque director, actor, and character • The deconstruction and reconstruction of a modern self-referential myth • The deconstruction of the biblical canon • Brechtian distancing from one's own narrative viewpoint • Textualist pre-inscription of the roles of discourse • The method of generating textualist-oneiric prose • The procedure of "faux scenes" • Political parable and biblical parable

Literary criticism and history have ascertained, albeit belatedly, the declaredly textualist poetic of the three-part novella entitled "Înscenare" ["A Staging"], published in its first version in 1967.[83]

83 The short story "Înscenare," first published in Romanian in *Gazeta literară*, no. 40, October 5, 1967, 4–5, is a triptych made up of "Maria de la şcoala normală" [Maria from the Normal School], "Patimile unui autor de teatru" [The Passion of a Playwright] and "Epilog." The first part was published, with the title "Maria de la Şcoala Medie" [Maria from the Middle School], in the volume Frig [Cold], but the other two parts were censored. The text of the novella was published in its entirety in the volume *Înscenare şi alte texte* [*A Staging and Other Texts*], with an afterword by Nicolae Oprea (Piteşti: Editura Calende, 1992). In the volume *Prin gaura cheii* [*Through the Keyhole*], the novella is included in the cycle "Înscenare," in which the narrative triptych is preceded by the text "Fuga" [Fugue, or: Flight] and followed by two epilogues:

However, Tsepeneag's textualism allows itself to be infused by the constant pathos of the authorial character, and is far from sharing the deliberately cold, "academic" tone and apparently neutral, dictionary-entry style specific to the textual exercise of Mircea Horia Simionescu in *Ingeniosul bine temperat* [*The Well-Tempered Ingenioso*], for example.[84] The playwright character in "A Staging," the same character as the director of the play included in the text *Nunta din Galateea* [*The Wedding in Galatea*], displays human/pre-human "passions," complexes, anxieties, caprices and idiosyncrasies compared with the actor characters. The supposedly typical textualist *coldness* (specific not only to the abovementioned representative of the Tîrgovişte School, but also to some of the later textualists, those of the Eighties Generation), the apparent lack of emotion with which the narratological theories and strategies of textual self-generation are exposited, sometimes ends up being drowned out by the often desperate confession of the "wretched" author character: "When an author realizes that he has deceived himself with regard to his characters, that they have got out of his control and are moving around of their own free will, it is not exactly pleasant. The author deflates like a balloon pricked by a sharp nib and perhaps might even lose faith in himself. Which is to say, he might tear up everything he has written. Especially if he has entertained too many illusions about his own authority."

"Variantă de epilog" [Variant of an Epilogue] and "Epilog în cîrciumă" [Epilogue in a Tavern].

84 The first volume, entitled *Dicționar onomastic*, in Mircea Horia Simionescu's tetralogy was published in 1969, and so Tsepeneag's textualist program in "A Staging" precedes it, even if it remained without any echo at the moment of its publication.

Accompanying and sometimes overwhelming his inclination toward self-derision, the lament of the textual playwright feeds on an obsessive anxiety regarding the Pirandello-esque emancipation[85] of his fictional creatures from their creator: "A protagonist enters the stage too early, another laughs when he should be crying, shows himself to be more despairing than is allowed to him or even dies, just like that, unexpectedly, he exits the stage just when the reader was getting used to him. What can the poor author do then? After he tears up what he has written, the others die too, it is the end, the void." The leitmotif of the character who has becomes "the magician's apprentice," a betrayer of his own creator, will also be found in the example of the author protagonist in the Romanian trilogy *Hotel Europa*, *Pont des Arts*, and *Maramureş*: "In vain did I strive to make my characters accomplices or even friends. I felt increasingly alone and, on top of it all, ridiculous" ("A Staging").

A director and at the same time dramatist, affectively unstable, fragile and suspicious of his own textual creations, the narrator of "A Staging" gives himself up to spectacular demiurgic phantasms. The imaginary scene of their unfolding seems an archetypically mimed frame, one of ultimately ostentatious artificiality, like an antique engraving: "It was a blue, gleaming,

85 Tsepeneag, like Ionesco before him, confesses to a Pirandello-esque split awareness of self, and as an author is an adept of the humorous and of frequent self-mirroring textual gestures: "I am acting in a theater play—I don't see how I can escape this Pirandello-esque mindset—a rather absurd play, and the fiction, which is my life, can confer additional value on the other fiction, that of the work;" see the diary entry for April 11, 1971, in *Un roman la Paris. Pagini de jurnal* [*A Romanian in Paris. Journal Pages*], third, definitive edition (Bucharest: Editura Cartea Românească, 2006), 141.

fresh morning. I cannot describe it. A morning that has returned from who knows when." The simulation a mythical, primordial atmosphere creates a visibly parodic mystification/mythicizing, in essence a deconstruction of the myth of the demiurge, of the maker of fictional worlds, and of his own textual and scenographic cosmogony. It is in a similarly faux archetypal scene, cobbled together from stage props, that the director/narrator of the short story "Pentru un album" ["For an Album"] makes his entrance. The story is a miniature parable, related, thanks to its textualist ending, to "Staging." Here, the principal director within the scene of the text is the old man with a crossbow, a vaguely grotesque Cupid. And the secondary director, who wants to save the pre-adolescent couple, by cutting them out of the "photograph" of the fictional landscape and thereby immortalizing them, is the author character himself, or, to be more exact, that willful, boastful, apparently capricious and at the same time vulnerable "I" that betrays its own anxieties regarding the void, the abyss, the *black hole* behind the text/image: "And then the idea came to me. I stood up, went towards them, pulled out the scissors and quickly, but carefully, began to cut them out. I cut them out of the landscape complete with the bench and some foliage behind. A leaf of darkness was left behind, into which I did not have the courage to look." Entering the fictional stage set, the voice that directs the characters—now mere puppets, devoid of depth, easily excisable from the "landscape"—denounces the old convention of lifelikeness as sleight of hand, and thereby undermines the supposed "reality" and referential consistency of the world behind the curtain or frame of the text. This is a possible world, which, however, leaves behind only a photographic print, i.e. an ontological simulacrum, a trace or shadow, an embodied illusion.

*

Also a simulacrum of a living being, an incarnate illusion, or rather a grotesque artifact is the rubber doll in "A Staging," that anguished, reified creature to which the character named, by no means randomly, Maria gives birth. The re-inscription of the biblical story of the Nativity of Christ has a clearly Urmuzian flavor: accompanied by Iosif, the Madonna is impregnated by no less than a bicycle pump, with which the one who calls himself, sometimes haughtily, sometimes in self-denigration, the Author "blows her up": "Every morning, I would sneak into Maria's room with the bicycle pump. At last, I felt I was a genuine author once more." Suspected of imposture and charlatanism by the host of ungrateful characters—former or future proselytes—the narrator, alias the director within the text, claims not only to be "the Author" par excellence, but also projects himself, phantasmically, as a kind of Christ caught up in the whirlwind of a biblical scene that has lapsed into derision. Consequently, he casts himself in the role of the Savior, adopting the script of the New Testament, but not without giving himself up to stupefying cynicism toward the disciples, as well as to not exactly Christian paranoid delusions of power and a strange, Brechtian distance towards his own role:

> The audience was hypnotized, they hung on my every word, they insatiably imbibed my words . . . They thrust forks into the imaginary flesh of my words, and the wine of faith and love gurgled down throats dry with emotion.
>
> "Love one another," I cried, masticating a large chunk of bloody flesh.
>
> "Live as brothers, for you are all episodic characters, nothing more. The author alone is immortal."

Although *alone*, unique in his culturally archetypical *immortality*, the Author has both the prerogatives of the Father, who inseminates Maria with the aid of a bicycle pump, and those of the Son. It is thanks to him that the gentle Maria gives birth. And it is the same confessional "I" of the narrator director, crucified like a Christ by the actors in his own play, who in the end recognizes her as his own grieving mother, or as a mother who acts out maternal grief: "I can no longer see Maria, I ache, mother, my screams, drowned out by the brass band, no longer reach you, you're weeping, which is to say, you're pretending to, you don't know that you genuinely ought to weep even if you did give birth to me more in jest, with the aid of a bicycle pump, and all of you, all you unfortunates, grunting for joy, standing on chairs, you too ought to weep and I pity you, you are killing the Author, you don't know what you're doing, oh!" The circularity of the text/Author relation, the verisimilar "staging"—authentic acting, "real" actors, fictionalized spectators, themselves transformed into characters—is exemplary, as in the different logical (and ontological) aporia of the Achilles and the tortoise paradox, or the ultra-clichéd paradox of the chicken and the egg. The author-director is the Father, he conceives the text, the scenario, then he finds, via Iosif, the actress for the part of the Madonna, he is the "midwife" of the performance, he reconfirms the quasi-mystical—or textualist, to be more precise—role of the Father, impregnating the virgin. He then ritually returns to the same pre-written existential circle, to claim the role of the Son, of Maria's infant, of the Savior crucified on/by his text, by his own characters, by his proselytes.

In Tsepeneag's "A Staging," Pontius Pilate becomes "comrade Chilate," who advises the author-director, the very actor who is playing Jesus, to declare, under interrogation by the militia, that everything was a practical joke, that the nativity and its mise-en-scène concealed nothing more than the usual theatrical or cinematic "effects." Mary Magdalene here becomes Magda the "tart." The author is also surrounded by "comrades" Pavelescu, Petrişor, the doubting old man Tomiţă, but also the traitor Iuga, who will turn him in to the militia. And in front of the virginal Maria, who gives birth to rubber dolls, three wise men from the east come to pay homage, "three respectable gentlemen with top hats, umbrellas and arms laden with gifts," devotees of the manners of the modern dandy.

The encounter between the author/Savior and the Devil is constructed not so much in a biblical as much as a "modern" spirit, rendered in an ironic, detached, literary tone. The arrival of the Devil, à la Bulgakov, "a short gentleman, dressed in black clothes with a greenish shine from long wear," takes place in a derisory, urban setting: the seemingly *atemporal,* abandoned park, alternately fascinating and squalid. This is a recurrent *topos* in the short prose of Dumitru Tsepeneag, even if we recall only the texts "Amintire" ["Reminiscence"], "Porumbela," "Pentru un album" ["For an Album"], and "Plînsul" ["The Weeping"]. As if at the circus, the children playing with their mothers or governesses gather fascinated around the Author and enjoy his stale, pathetic conjuring tricks. The Devil is greeted with annoyance and scorn by the author/conjurer, who experiences around this suspect creature an insidious feeling of déjà vu ("I knew who it was," he remarks). The *Messire* with the "cracked," infernal voice teases his latest victim: "You've made a fool of yourself, even in front of these stupid children and women. You've made a fool of yourself. A fine author you are! What'll you do on the stage, how are you going to save your bacon? Ha, ha . . . an author!" Censoring his creative hubris with biting sarcasm, the Devil accuses him, moreover, of chronic boredom, of existential disgust, he confiscates his "work," his notebook of texts, to be more precise, and challenges him to prove, by acts of quasi-magic, that he and only he is the authentic author. He even tries to tempt him, in a parody of the Faustian pact, with the promise that he might grant him the ability to fly.

The scene of this encounter with a Romanian Woland or Korovyev is imbued with a programmatic textualism. The Mephistophelean collocutor of the author-character suspects the latter of being in the habit of writing the text as he goes along, as he "acts" or performs on the stage, in other words as he "lives." The author is supposed always to *pre-write* the scene that is apparently unfolding, under the very eyes of the reader/audience. The idea of directing/conceiving a text step by step, with each passage or scene being pre-written in the instant that comes immediately before, in fact almost concomitantly with the unfolding "drama" of the play, recalls "Marea amărăciune" ["The Great Disappointment"], a textualist novella by Eighties Generation writer Ioan Groşan. In the story, the protagonists, Sebastian Pop and Ioana, pre-write even the most insignificant lines in their love story, apparently being incapable of living intensely outside the ludic adventure of pre-writing their own lives, which is in the end comes to be touched by bitterness. The self-mirroring text of "A Staging" by Dumitru Tsepeneag thus anticipates by almost a decade the textualist game to be found in the novellas of Groşan (published in this first collection of prose, entitled *Caravana cinematografică* [*The Cinema Caravan*], in 1985, which includes "O dimineaţă minunată pentru proză scurtă" ["A Wonderful Morning for a Short Story"], "Insula" ["The Island], "Caravana cinematografică" ["The Cinema Caravan"] and "Marea amărăciune" ["The Great Disappointment"], originally published between 1971 and 1981 in student magazines *Echinox* and *Amfiteatru*). The dialogue between the Author and the diabolical buffoon in "A Staging," a mise en abyme of the self-generating mechanism of the text, is relevant for the leading place Dumitru Tsepeneag's short prose has held in the history of Romanian textualism over the last few decades:

> "Is there anything written about me in that notebook?"
> I regarded him calmly and scornfully.
> "There is. More than plenty. Quite enough!"
> "All right, but is this scene written there, too? Eh? Is it or isn't it written there? . . .

> The scene has gone on a bit too long and for this, naturally, I am the one to blame, but as it's an important scene I can't really cut it.

In the cultural and mythological palimpsest interwoven among the pages of the authorial "staging," there is also a political parable. Imbued with parody, the textual weft of ideological and propagandistic discourse underlies the parable of biblical creation and that of the author-savior. These discourses consume and diabolically reflect one another. The lines of the author character often subvert the censorship that the "militia," an instrument of political power, exerts over the spiritual "birth" of literary, theatrical creation. Entire passages can be read as allusions to the cultural censorship of the recently ended Stalinist period, but also as astonishing premonitions, given that the text was published in 1967, of the cultural morass that was to be produced by Ceauşescu's July Theses of 1971. The third version of the epilogue, entitled "Epilog în cîrciumă" ["Epilogue in a Tavern"], even includes a parody of the cultural propaganda of the Ceauşescu period. It is a pseudo-discourse enunciated by the militiaman, who himself has become—as if by a cruel practical joke played by history—an author, apparently convinced of the need to ideologize art, to make it subservient to political power, zealously pronouncing himself in favor of socialist-realist theater, "one both modern and healthy." The voice of the director character remains incorruptible and "prickly," however, eternally rebelling against the abuses of censorship:

> I have to shout to make myself heard:
>
> "I cannot, comrade colonel, I cannot make concessions."
>
> This is the play and I will perform it to the very end.

The later anti-totalitarian parable told by playwright Matei Vişniec in his well-known *Spectatorul condamnat la moarte* [*The Audience Member Condemned to Death*] is seemingly anticipated in "A Staging" by the dialogue of the recalcitrant author arrested by the head of the militia:

> "Ultimately, of what am I accused? Because I am an author?"
>
> It's stupid . . .
>
> "They say that you're not an author. You're not a member of the Authors' Union."

The atmosphere of "Epilogue in a Tavern," with its subversive comical bonhomie, reminiscent of Caragiale's skits, with interminable discussions between whimsical customers and bored waiters nodding off in their chairs, gradually takes on darker colors and is pervaded with theatrical trickery set in motion by means of a mysterious, absurdist textual mechanism. It functions, in its immanence, over the heads of the characters, vampirizing them, speaking through them, manipulating them thanks to a directorial power of occult provenance. One of proselytes of the deceased author recalls the latter's faith in the "necessity of the absurd." Invoking the author as a Savior, whose sole imposture would be no more than the sublime act of having risen from the dead (Magda, for example, "says she saw him," "she says that he is among us"), the actor-evangelists verbally duel with each other, in dialogue that recalls now Urmuz, now Ionesco. The mythologized portrait the author-director paints of him blends elements from the real biography of the "character" Tsepeneag (it seems that either he is in Paris, or that he has not yet obtained a passport "from on high") with his supposed characteristics of oneiric ubiquity. This faux dialogue is paralogical, reminiscent of plays such as *L'Anglais sans peine* or *La Cantatrice chauve*:

> "He was seen at the market."
>
> "At the market?"
>
> "Yes, in the guise of a shepherd" . . .
>
> "Later he was seen in a jar."
>
> "A jar?"
>
> "He was directing the traffic."
>
> "Extraordinary! He's a genius!"
>
> "He wouldn't let anything pass!"
>
> "Of course" . . .
>
> "What a person!" exclaims Luca with pathos.
>
> "He did have talent, that's true," says old man Tomiță.
>
> "Do you remember the performance with the wedding?" . . .
>
> "What elegant gestures he made . . . as if he were moving wings instead of arms. He was tall . . ."
>
> "He was short and rather fat," insists old man Tomiță.
>
> "He was handsome," continues Luca, looking at the militiaman.

"His nose was too big . . . small, beady eyes."
"He was a perfect orator."

The scene of the pseudo-dialogue à la Ionesco is symptomatic of the dual artistic typology to be found in the work of Dumitru Tsepeneag, which implies not only self-castigating derision but also a narcissistic, phantasmic projection of self, by means of textual roles or masks, which are half fictional, half autobiographical.

*

On the other hand, the above-quoted anti-theater sequence within the epic "A Staging"—a "faux scene," as Tsepeneag would call it—is also relevant with regard to the method whereby the oneiric/textualist writer's later texts are generated and structured. In a dialogue with Laurențiu Ulici in the margins of the "oneiric" novel *Serenadă la trompetă* [*Serenade on a Trumpet*] by Sânziana Pop, Dumitru Tsepeneag theorizes precisely the procedure of "faux scenes," as they are called by Bruce Morrissette in his book about Alain Robbe-Grillet.

Faux in fact implies artificiality of method. Tsepeneag considers that the author acquires a position similar to that of the director on the film set, because he can at any time make a cut in the unfolding action or point to *false leads*, designed to create fertile ambiguity. A meta-narrative situation symptomatic as regards ambiguity and faux scenes occurs in "Ciorile" ["The Crows"], a short story with a textualist ending from 1970. Here, a voice alienated from itself is heard, as if from the off-stage of the split textual consciousness, berating the "I" for its choice of ending: "You can't end like this.

There are two things that contradict each other. If you're set on the final part, you'll just have to redo it, rewrite it all over again, separately." And the voice of the supposed author of the text within the text, irritated by the incomprehension of an imaginary reader, ripostes with defiantly ludic words, rather in the same fashion as the young Ionesco in his short narcissistic text entitled "Eu" ["I"]: "That's right. But I'm also set on the first part. I'm set on both parts. I must say once and for all, and I'll scream it if you don't understand, that I'm set on both parts . . . Even if they don't go together. What I am supposed to do in that case? Even if in the end I still have to tear myself in two, to gouge one of my eyes out, to rip off an arm, a leg, an ear. Let the world think I'm a one-eared madman. But which?" The ludic textual director may even invoke an arbitrary note, to contradict the lifelikeness of the action. This is because in modern prose the relationship to reality does not arise homologically, as it does in the traditional aesthetic of *mimesis*, but analogically. In the reality conventionally designated as "real" only the objectively material can be found, but not the laws of aesthetic construction. Moreover, "through this procedure of faux scenes, the author too becomes a character, the same as the director in Fellini's *8½*.[86] Similarly, in Sânziana Pop's novel the psychological dissipates and even disappears, or it is at most implied in the gestures, action and drama of the novel, becoming a kind of *narrated movie*.

Tsepeneag the theorist thus seems to be characterizing in a masked way, *in nuce*, anti-psychologizing, visually dynamic, screenplay-like writing. But he is also heralding what I might

---

86 See *Luceafărul*, no. 23, 7 July 1969, 6–7.

name the oblique, "faux" lighting of the narrative viewpoint in a number of his subsequent major novels. For example, *Novel for Reading on the Train*, where the author-director is a pedantically faithful reincarnation, in terms of typology, of the one in the earlier "A Staging." Likewise, *Hotel Europa* and *La belle Roumaine* are simultaneously cinematic epics and self-mirroring texts.

The oblique narrative angle, programmed artificiality, discursive refraction • I/him: narrative roles and phantasms, specular imaginary worlds • The imaginary double and twin • Mise en abyme and complementary fictional levels: the mirror, the dream, the painting • Discursive arpeggios and traps • A textual, pictorial, musical, theatrical, cinematic performance piece • The category of the miraculous and the "technique" of prose • The breach between fictionality and textuality

The premeditated *artificiality* of Dumitru Tsepeneag's prose is an appendage of the author's directorial freedom, with all its dose of oneiric miraculousness. But it is an artificiality that also betrays an *oblique* narrative viewpoint, calculated according to a precise angle of the authorial gaze relative to the text he is about to create. Many of the short stories of the author's youth, collected in the volumes *Exercises*, *Cold*, and *Waiting*, result from a process of *discursive refraction*, detectable also in the later novels. The refraction, rather than merely the reflection, of the voices audible in the text takes place in stages. Firstly, the voice that emits the text, more often than not in the *first person*, transgresses the traditional boundary of the conventions of lifelikeness and epic omniscience. Then, too, the narrator "I" penetrates the reflective surface of the text, like beams of light entering the mirroring surface of water, and metamorphoses into the *third person singular.* The textualization of this fascinating catoptrical play of refracting narrative perspectives can also be reversed: *he* becomes *I* once more, or a third-party, supra-textual *I* or *He*, engulfed by the other partial narrative instances.

The short sketch "El" ["He"] in the volume *Cold*, a text of splendid formal asceticism, a kind of "sonnet in prose," has a *he* for its primary subject, that of the fictional evocation, and an *I* as its secondary subject or supra-subject, a voice that gives birth to the evocation and determines the discursive atmosphere: "He was as handsome and tall as a plume of smoke. He was sitting on the edge of the bed, motionless, his hands clasped between his knees. His smile had frozen on his lips. I liked him." The first-person narrator gives himself up to the silent, occult spell of the other, and naïvely tries to "cheer him up," to stir some kind of reaction in him: "And I know that he was not looking at me . . . Around him the air was quivering, disturbing his rigid, delicate outline. His face was stone-like and wax like at the same time." But the hieratic character *He*—interpreted by Romanian critic Valeriu Cristea[87] as a Christ-like figure—belongs to a different order of textual generation, one that

87 *Interpretări critice* [*Critical Interpretations*] (Bucharest: Editura Cartea Românească, 1970), 130.

is to a certain extent occult. This other, supra-textual order, which pre-writes *His* destiny, also sacrifices him, in a seemingly ritualistic way, leaving him prey to serpents. *He* is strangled, and therefore the fictional character is, as it were, killed out of inter-textual necessity, in order to accomplish the virtualities of a text imbued with cultural signs, with mythemes (the textual matrix being the myth of Laocoön). The *I* in the end becomes a helpless witness to the sacrifice of the other. And his pain, the "weakness" of his subjective lamentation, in the first person, remains outside the Text in which the Other is the real protagonist. It is by no means aleatory that this *I* is metaphorically situated in the age of childhood. For the *I* cannot yet pierce through the density of the voices and various levels of *textual consciousness*—or rather textualist consciousness—to reach the *He*. Thus, to the point of absolute, perhaps divine alterity: "He remained silent. He was not looking at me. I could no longer control myself. I began to weep, there beneath the piano, with muffled sobs, for I was ashamed for him to discover my weakness."

The same problematic *I/he* relationship is the mechanism that triggers the fictional texture, but also a complex process that artificially lights the various textual voices, in the short story "The Weeping." Here, the *he* is a kind of infra-being, belonging to an indefinite realm: "But he was neither an eagle nor a lion, because he was weeping. And nor was he a man, although the dreadfully thin, emaciated body seemed human." An incarnation of a different, mirrored consciousness of the *I*, its *double*, in the post-romantic sense, or a personal *angel*, the *he* seemingly takes upon his shoulders the narrator's affective decay and anxieties and *weeps* endlessly. Moreover, this *he* has mysterious motives—

shame, remorse, guilt or resentment—not to allow himself always to be *seen* or brought into being by the gaze of the *I*. In other words, not to be visible to the first person *subject* that is situated in the affective position of the Father, as well as the narratological "director" of the text.

The *I* on the other hand resorts to dream in order to confirm its vocation as demiurge of the fiction in which the protagonist is the *he*, as a possible phantasmic embodiment of the weeping: "I would hear in my sleep his muffled weeping and sobs, and I would see the backs of his hands puckered with the two scars, the two round, brown coins, I would see how he covered his eyes: for, he did not want to see me and I would have to dream him—what great efforts!—to see his face in my dream, the sad eyes, on rare occasions happy (. . .) to make him, at least in the dream, stop the weeping." The oneiric imagery will more than once be instrumentalized in order to direct the existential gestures and attitudes of the other, of the *he*. But why is it essential for the apparently much more fulfilled *I* to keep a close watch over the inner splitting of the other? In any case, the profound, subliminal dependence of the *I* on the avatars of its alterity, projected onto the third person as its strange and alienated *he*, remains self-evident, as though dating from the beginning of the world. The relationship is reversible, and the *alter ego* sometimes even seems to have a greater hypnotic power over the *ego*. The *he* in its turn directs the oneiric text of the *I*, confounding the unfolding script written by the supposed demiurge. And this demiurgic first-person subject comes to be contaminated by the alienation and the chronic weeping of its character: "The scenes get mixed up, they combine with each other. I want to escape, and I also want to escape from this unbearable weeping, I feel my face with my hands, my forehead, my cheeks are damp, and then I bury my face in the pillow to weep or to go on dreaming."

The propensity of the narrator *I* to perceive specular worlds and existences, to reduplicate itself as *Me* and *Him*, is also transcribed in its passion for photography. This passion is also amplified by the sight of the other, by the realization of surprising similarity with the other. The *I* of "The Weeping" discovers itself mirrored in the image and existential trajectory of the other, as though it had a revelation of what psychoanalyst Wilfred R. Bion refers to as the *imaginary twin.*[88] The following passage from "The Weeping" is relevant in this sense: "I used to see him now and then, passing on a bicycle, we were both very young back then . . . I was a photographer's assistant, I had learned to develop photographs and even to retouch them. Many times I lay in wait for him, to photograph him as he passed haughtily on his bicycle or, thinking himself to be alone, as he summoned from who knows whence a silvery-grey eagle, which perched on his shoulder or his knees, digging its powerful claws into his flesh. It is true that he did like to have his photograph taken." On the one hand, the *other,* the *he*, "thinks he is alone," therefore he projects himself as the sole *I.* On the other hand, he discovers in his turn that he has a different *other*, which confirms to him, by an extension of self, his identity, in the form of the eagle that arrives from a stupendous Anti-World in the Ionesco vein. Moreover, the same *he* also gets the idea of founding

88 See Wilfred R. Bion, *Second Thoughts. Selected Papers on Psycho-Analysis* (London: William Heineman Medical Books Ltd., 1967).

a traveling theater, an obsession common to other narrator characters, this time first-person voices, in other prose pieces by Tsepeneag (for example, in "A Staging"). The hallucinatory slippage or catoptric play of *I/he/eagle*, in which the identity of each becomes hybrid, brings with it the ambiguity of the various levels of specularity in the text: the dream or reminiscence, or the fictional story proper, seem to transgress their boundaries and merge together: "So many things have happened, some of them perhaps did not really happen, perhaps I merely dreamed them, or I am dreaming them now, or I heard them being recounted by others. I cannot remember them all, many have been lost or have faded like photographs kept in sunlight for a long time . . ."

In addition, the *he* will be crucified, the sacrifice conferring upon him, as it did upon the directorial *I* in "A Staging," the destiny of a prosaic Christ, whose derisoriness nevertheless unites with the sublime. The text's mise en abyme sequences are multiplied, the concentric circles of the successive levels at which the textual processes occur are deepened: the narrator *I* invokes the other, the *he*, as a character now in a position almost identical to the figure in Magritte's painting *Le mal du pays*. His nakedness seems to be a sign of his existential essence, of his archetypal nature. And the lion is just as much an alter ego as the eagle at other times. The mirror represented by the dream, by the oneiric surface, combined with the "mirror" of the painting, which once again *met en abyme* the text as a whole, ensures the permeability of identities, the interchangeability of *I/he*. The imagery might be compared to another painting by René Magritte, entitled *Decalcomania*, in which the outline of the back of a man wearing a suit and a bowler hat (but not a top hat like Tsepeneag's characters) is accompanied, shoulder to shoulder, by his negative image, as if by an *imaginary twin*.

The narrator, who oscillates between dream and waking, the same as the director who edits the film of the text, traverses, thanks to the oneiric trance, a number of strata of existence, a number of *possible worlds*. But these reveal themselves to him jumbled up in a jigsaw puzzle of scenes, in a surreality characterized by temporal simultaneity, whose sole point of reference and leitmotif is *he*: "The scenes repeat themselves, join together, but with the top hat on his head the eagle too jabs the frail breast with its beak . . . the images whirl together and I have to make an effort to wake up. But do I wake up? For, I do not hear the weeping, I raise myself on my elbows, prick up my ears, wait . . ." In the short story entitled "Dor de patrie" ["Homesickness"], Tsepeneag resorts once again to an *ekphrasis* of the painting of the same title by Magritte. In the Anti-World of the specular space of the painting can be found both the *I* and the *he*. Making his confession to a quasi-imaginary *she* who seems to have left him, the protagonist, as the text's primary voice, in the first person (". . . you abandoned me in that hotel room full of bedbugs . . ."), repeats the destiny of the other, of the secondary character, the one imprisoned in the fictional frame of the painting. Or in the frame of the narrative, of recollection, of dream: "He had been abandoned here, in who knows what hotel room full of bedbugs, there was nothing else he could do, every morning he looked at his ever filthier wings, the top hat, the newspaper lying by the armchair, the shoes . . ."

Another mise-en-abyme scene in the short story "Homesickness," which, I think, permits supra- or meta-textual interpretation, is the narrator's (and, of course, his double's) contemplation of the most infinitesimal motions of seawater: "I was walking and watching how the waves grew smaller and smaller, until they withdrew, and how as the sun sank on the other side the sea grew paler and a fine mist, more and more visible, settled from the horizon over the whitening liquid expanse; it was like steam, like the panting breath of the sea . . ." Ultimately, the specular surface of the textual "sea" is also traversed by as many delicate breezes and in its turn lets itself be enveloped by the misty steam of an ambiguous, polyphonically orchestrated meaning. To see in the encompassing image of the sea a metaphor—albeit one nestling in the creative unconscious, imbued with signs—for the text is not entirely arbitrary. And this is because Tsepeneag's suspicion, consonant with but also independent of that of the French nouveau roman authors, of traditional aesthetic boundaries, as well as of those established by convention between various types of prose, is well known. The ebbs and flows of the aquatic, (self-)mirroring, continually reflective text overflow any such rigid boundaries.[89]

89 A subtle observation with regard to the way in which Tsepeneag's writing, centered on the domino principle and the technique of counterpoint, transcends the dichotomy between aesthetic formalism and the expressionism of Derrida's "transcendental signifiers" is made by Georgiana Lungu Badea: "Puisque l'écriture de Tsepeneag ne véhicule pas des significations comptables et échangeables, elle résiste à la dégradation en signes. Son écriture procède du principe du domino et de la technique du contrepoint et rende, de la sorte, caduque la bipolarisation instaurée entre le formalisme esthétique—musical ou pictural—, hypothétiquement abstrait et non référentiel, et l'expressionnisme de formes idéales et extérieures, nommés 'signifiés transcendantaux.'" "L'architecture processuelle d'une oeuvre: théorisations, pratiques, interférences dans l'oeuvre de Dumitru Tsepeneag," in *Dumitru Tsepeneag. Les Métamorphoses d'un créateur: écrivain, théoricien, traducteur. Les actes du colloque organisé les 14–15 avril 2006, avec la participation de l'écrivain*, ed. Georgiana Lungu Badea, Margareta Gyurcsik (Timişoara : Editura Universităţii de Vest, 2006), 60.

The mysterious person dressed in a smoking jacket, possessor of wings and a miraculous totemic lion, tries to escape by flight, to liberate himself from the role pre-written for him in the text-fiction. He can, ultimately, also be read as a phantasmic figuration or as an eternally deceptive pseudo-incarnation of *meaning*. A faceless figure, positioned with his back to the viewer, the same as in the Magritte painting, the *I's other* originates from a "homeland" beyond the painting or the text. An inverted, thanatic world. He may merely belong to a different level of "reality," or, contrariwise, to another, enhanced level of fictionality. In the phantasm of the narrator, his impenetrable alter ego has to cry out in order to claim for himself, with desperate pride, any *difference* in ontological realm: "I'm not from here! I'm not from here!" Nevertheless, the *he* cannot in the end elude the trap of the text in which he has been born, always returning, in a ritualistic movement, flying in concentric circles, to the matrix, in the imaginary (intra- and inter-textual) space to which he rightly belongs: "And even if he had tried to fly . . . after describing a circle, then another, a little lower, ever lower circles, I am sure he would have returned, perhaps without his top hat, which would have made him, if not more ridiculous, then in any case nondescript. The top hat had its purpose." (Often, the purpose of this apparently whimsical item of attire is to mark yet again, paradoxically, through a *double* contrast of objects, the subjectivity and the consistency of the largely autobiographical fictional outlines in Tsepeneag's prose, conferring upon them an extra note of aristocratic, *belle époque* distinction and melancholic dandyism). In the profoundest textualist spirit, the voice of the primary subject, of the narrator *I*—having momentarily become demiurgic once again—immediately adds, in connection with the customary top hat: "But I've grown used to it . . ."

Should the character wear a top hat or not? Should he disappear for good or return ad hoc? Should he make Sisyphean attempts to fly or should he give up on his bovarist fantasies and sink back into the ridiculousness and derisoriness of the everyday (as in the sketch "Icarus")? It is the right of the Author-director, be he arbitrary, despotic or merely humble toward his creations, to decide.

*

In *Arpièges* [*Vain Art of the Fugue*], the young man who is running to catch a train, clutching a bunch of flowers, accumulates both the role of a quasi-impersonal *he* and that of a somewhat more empathetic, even slightly pathetic, *I*, but one capable of doubling himself and looking at himself from the outside. The hybrid *he/I* subject becomes a figure of the agglutinating imaginary thanks to the musically inspired textual strategy of the *fugue*.[90] The polyphonic textual ebbs and flows bring with them at times an apparently distanced perspective, like a camera panning in a circle, of the image of a *he* in motion, and at other times a voice marked by the albeit still amorphous subjectivity of an *I*: "I'm already late

90 B. Caron writes as follows in *Études* (May, 1973) in connection with the textualized music of the novel: "Art et piège, arpège – le calembour musical est volontairement révélateur de cet art nouveau qui est critique de l'art romanesque passé ou en voie de l'être, autocritique où le récit éclate en pluriel thématique, variation et exploitation de gammes et d'accords, où la succesivité traditionelle du récit composé perd toute dimension ou épaisseur chronologique pour devenir reprises, ébauches musicales travaillées et réitérées."

and don't feel like rushing from platform to platform (you never know exactly which one to wait on), running around with my coat unbuttoned and tails flapping . . . there's no point shouting or waving your bunch of flowers like a flag, faster and faster in that huge, reddish, thick-veined hand, while the train disappears at the end of the platform," "Now he saw the stop and broke into a run. He managed to catch the bus right at the last moment," "The bus started up again and then the woman made a sign to me with her hand. To me? Yes, why not?" "The woman continues to look vacantly towards the man; he has turned the corner, hurriedly strides along with his head slightly bent, rather awkwardly clutching a bunch of flowers." The female characters, Maria and Magda (Marie and Madeleine, in French), ascribable to the same biblical archetype, Mary Magdalene, make up a two-headed creature, with a self-mirroring hybrid identity that is successively split and reunited. The *I/he* protagonist sets off towards one of them only to reach the other, and vice versa. There is, here, an art of the fugue, a circular or even spiral unfolding of arpeggios with narrative traps (as the etymology of the hybrid vocable *arpièges*, made up of "arpèges" and "pièges," would suggest). It imbues the textual breezes and those of the imagery with a paradoxical motionless motion, which recalls Zeno of Elea's famous aporia of Achilles and the tortoise. Similarly, French critic Daniel Oster, who classes Tsepeneag's novelistic *arpèges* as being equal in value to the most important achievements of Claude Simon and Claude Ollier, calls the book "Zeno of Elea's first novel."[91] The inter-textual

91 "Sans doute serait-on tenté de rapprocher Arpièges des meilleurs réussites de Claude Simon ou, mieux encore, de Claude Ollier" (see "Le premier roman de Zénon d'Elée," in *Les Nouvelles Littéraires*, November 24–December 1, 1973).

references are visibly woven, with sophisticated literary irony, into the textual and allegorical fabric of the novel: the maieutics of the train mechanic and conductor concerning the ancient aporetic parable about the impossibility of motion, as well as the presence of characters such as the child Zenon or Pamfile (alias Achilles), an athlete who catches the tortoise, but only because it is sleeping.

The narrative, or, rather, descriptive, perspective verifies the theoretical "truth" formulated by Jean Ricardou regarding "the anti-realist effect of description" and "simultaneity in successiveness" in the nouveau roman. This is a continually relativized perspective of textual *fugue* or flight, but also the eternal, circular flight of the interchangeable identities of those who view the panorama of the text. Various nameless characters, one-dimensional *fantoches*, simultaneously playing the role of actors and audience, enter the moving spiral of the text, in order to describe themselves and their own point of view and development. For example, the cyclist with the striped shirt and top hat, who continually pedals, transporting some fish in his pannier, is an apparently secondary character, an easily manipulated textual marionette, a phantasm of the dual (*I/he*) narrator. But the figure of the cyclist might at any time take the narrative/descriptive initiative and be transformed from phantasmic being into creator and director of the other textual parts. His condition as an anthropomorphic film camera in continual motion is also characteristic of a number of Tsepeneag's other more markedly autobiographical characters: the narrator *I*, also in the guise of a cyclist, in "The Weeping," the director in "A Staging," who impregnates Maria with a bicycle pump, and the writer protagonist in the novel *Maramureș*, who pedals endlessly, wearing a magician's hat.

In the (non-)action, outlined by *arpièges* or discursive *traps*, the repeated stage entrances of the cyclist are thus by no means aleatory. They threaten to create a fissure in the text, which, progressively widening, will end up turning upside down the protagonists designated as *I* and *he*. The cyclist seems to want to replace them, to reduce them, from the height of his superior, cinematic perspective, to mere narrative "pedestrians," in order to accede to the formerly titular role of this *I* or *he*:

> He walked on the very edge of the pavement. A passing cyclist rode so close that he struck him with his shoulder; he tried to recover his balance by turning the handlebars left and right, so that a fish slipped from the rack and fell onto the asphalt as if into a little river. The cyclist pulled up and began to yell and curse. The walker stopped, put down the trunk and looked at where the tin-plate handle had reddened his palm and fingers. He shrugged his shoulders. He saw the fish slide off towards the middle of the road and then turn left, heading in the direction from which it had come. But the maneuver was unsuccessful: the cyclist saw it out of the corner of his eye and ran off to catch the fish after it had gone about twenty yards; he picked it up, of course, then returned triumphantly to his bicycle and looked around for the pedestrian, who had meanwhile slipped away to the opposite side of the road.

The discursive movements explain or encipher the figures of the imaginary, by means of metonymic textual drawings, cryptograms and ideograms. Even when the prose of Tsepeneag seems to contain a surplus of textualization and the epic substance is muted, the map described by the textual flux grounds it as an oneiric *reality*. The screen of the text as dream acquires a third and then a fourth dimension, as positive *absences*, in the Lacanian sense.

The textual/oneiric phantasms clash, superimpose, then return, slightly metamorphosed, brought back into the whirlpool of sentences, just like a fish—a familiar trans-human alter ego of Tsepeneag's characters—wandering free down the street. In one of his appearances, the cyclist resembles the father of the main character: ". . . a serious gentleman who looks a little like his father, although his father doesn't wear a jersey, never wore one in his life." The paternal archetype is also detectable in the figure of the old man released from prison. He boards the same train, whose function is likely that of a psychopomp.

At a given point, the clash of various phantasmic plot lines and leitmotifs appears to be willfully arbitrary, as if to emphasize that the sometimes complementary musical *themes*[92] of the novel nevertheless preserve their own autonomy. When, for example, the peaceful young man who is on his way to the station clashes with the parallel world, as if from a different fictional level, of the soldiers out of a war-film scenario, the astonishment of the persons involved is in keeping with the "accident." The pseudo-plot of the novel thus originates from apparently insignificant,

92 It should be remarked that as early as in the afterword, entitled "Tehnica fascinației" [The Technique of Fascination], to his translation of Alain Robbe-Grillet's novel, in Romanian *În labirint* [*In the Labyrinth*], Dumitru Tsepeneag argues for the musical character of this example of the nouveau roman. The musicality of Robbe-Grillet's prose is founded on two characteristics of the sentence, alternation and seriality, and "substantially contributes to the visual charge of the image." See *Momentul oniric*, 103.

infra-textual incidents, explainable only by means of the para-logic of a surreal Anti-World:

> Left, right, left . . . Now he felt two claws in the middle of his neck; streams of perspiration appeared on his forehead, trickling down into his eyes and past his ears, tickling the curve of his spine. He stopped.
>
> "What are you doing? Keep moving!" The boots of the soldiers in front continued to ring out on the cement. "Why did you stop?" A shout came from somewhere. He turned his head and saw the sergeant red with fury: come on, move, forward march!

Confronted with an *intruder*, teleported out of the blue into their sphere of action, as if through a portal in time, the soldiers are left perplexed. Their reaction makes no sense at the first level of novelistic convention, that of the simulacrum of fictional plot, but rather it can be justified only at the second, meta-textual level: "The other two soldiers stopped and looked back in astonishment."

In a diary entry dated 3/4 January 1971, the author makes revealing confessions about the sophisticated textualist method of his "art of the fugue" in the novel in progress to which he gave the provisional title *Fugue*:

> I have found the following structure for *Fugue*: an obstacle race—as in games for children; I select a number of obstacle-words and a number of obsession-words. As far as the obsession-words are concerned, it's simple:

they will probably be *hen* (hens), *hawk* (thus, a degradation of the symbolic eagle), and *dog* (parodically recalling a lion). Probably others as well . . . It will be a bit more complicated with the obstacle-words. The main character "runs" from one woman to another, from Magda to Maria, or vice versa; in fact, after a given point, you will no longer be able to tell. The fixed point is the train station where one of the women is about to arrive or from where she is about to leave. On his way to the station, the character will be "forced" to think, and he will also think of the obstacle-words, let's say the word *garden*; in that instant, he will find himself in a garden (or in a certain garden, thus another fixed or semi-fixed point) with the other woman, from where he will have to leave, to set off once more towards the station; he will head there using various means of transport (tram, bus, taxi) or even on foot, in flight. He is in a hurry, afraid of being late, but he can't stop himself thinking or stumbling on the word *seaside*, let's say, or beach; and so here he is on the beach with the other woman (after a given point it is no longer known which woman is at the station, as both their names are mentioned or, even worse, the initial letter, which is the same—M), from where he will set off yet again towards the station (Which station? It doesn't matter) without ever arriving.[93]

93 *Un român la Paris. Pagini de jurnal* [*A Romanian in Paris. Journal Pages*], 3rd, definitive edition, 79–80.

As if in a parody of a science-fiction screenplay, by uttering a certain word the character will fall victim to a transcendental practical joke. He is caught in the trap of a parallel world, brought into being by the ludic, quasi-magical invocation of the vocable in question.

Here, thinking is, in the Wittgensteinian sense, at the same time also language. And the word almost instantaneously becomes act, with utterance constituting, in the sense of J. L. Austin's linguistic philosophy, the principal performative incident that leads to the realization of an action. The creature of this textual *performance* in *Vain Art of the Fugue* ends up being teleported into another space-time dimension through the materialization at an imaginary level of his mental utterance. The strategy that triggers the textualist flow of the discourse consequently determines step by step the means whereby the micro-scenes and fictional phantasms are generated.

The constellations of phantasmic leitmotifs that spring from the frequent discursive traps have a compact, almost monadic character. Thanks to their autonomy, they can circulate not only throughout the novel but also in other, earlier or later, texts by Dumitru Tsepeneag. The image of the man slaughtering a pig, watched by some women, the metonymic sequence of the young boy playing with a train set, and also the leitmotif of war, to be found, among other texts, in *The Sandglass Word, Novel for Reading on the Train,* and *Maramureş*, are textual ectoplasms that overflow the apparent boundaries of the novel. Their proportion within the faux plot as a whole depends on the viewpoint of the character in question, who might in turn play the role of the director or audience within the text. The distance at which the witness is located, whether he is static or in motion, his degree of affective involvement in the scene under contemplation, is decisive. It would seem that the young man hurrying to get to the station involuntarily directs, by means of his fleeting glances, the scene of the repeated, obsessive stabbing of the pig by the driver. The sketch of a thriller-type scenario can be glimpsed here, and beneath the young man's eyes the scene acquires a pathological violence, which seemingly humanizes the sacrificial victim. Moreover, the "film camera" that is the man's gaze imbues the sequence[94] with a lyrical hue, as if in a paradoxical mise-en-scène molded according to oneiric "legislation":

> "For a remote observer—for example, that young man hurrying along with his comically big steps, holding a bunch of flowers so awkwardly that you'd think he was carrying a chicken from the market, a little frightened and disgusted—for such an observer, who stops to gawk with curiosity at what is, in the end, just a banal, everyday scene, it looks as though the driver continues to strike blindly with his dripping knife, driving it into the heap of flesh and blood-smeared garments, while the other

94 The following is the original version from *Arpièges* of the sequence of the stabbing of the pig, which antipates the apotheotic finale of the novel: "Pour un observateur éloigné, par exemple pour ce jeune homme qui marche d'un air pressé, en faisant des pas ridiculement grands, et qui tient un bouquet de fleurs de manière si gauche que l'on croirait qu'il porte une volaille achetée au marché, eh bien, pour celui-ci, qui fait halte, curieux de voir cette scène au fond banale, le chauffeur continue à frapper avec son couteau dégoulinant de sang, à le planter dans l'amas de chair et de vêtements poissés, tandis que les autres femmes s'échappent ou bien jettent leurs soupières, cherchent à arrêter le bras impitoyable de l'homme, l'une d'entre elles tombe à genoux, l'autre lève les bras au ciel et semble prier . . ."

> women run away or throw down their bowls and try to stay the man's pitiless hand, one of them falling on her knees, another raising her arms to heaven in a gesture of prayer . . ."

Nor is the scene lacking in the allure of a modern meta-film,[95] centered on the phantasm of a highly bloody pre-Christian ritual, whose hallucinatory violence is exploited with a kind of decadent sadism and a dose of amoral aestheticism à la Pier Paolo Pasolini. If the awkward young man in a hurry to get to the station can be interpreted as a partially autobiographical reflection of the author, an authorial character inside the fictional frame, then his profile as a sophisticated intellectual would permit such associations and presuppositions about his aesthetic tastes and choices.

The protagonist designated by the third person singular, the narrating *he* that captures in motion the expressionist tableau of the animal being slaughtered, is in his turn viewed through

95 Referring, in a diary entry in *A Romanian in Paris* dated October 28, 1971, to the scene of the slaughtering of the pig in Zenon—one of the provisory titles for the future novel *Arpièges/Zadarnică e arta fugii* [*Vain Art of the Fugue*]—Dumitru Tsepeneag enthusiastically admits to a propensity for cinematic technique. Like fellow nouveau roman author Alain Robbe-Grillet, whom he has translated and about whom he has written literary criticism, he has the idea of making a film. But what is important is to translate the cinematographic procedure into the writing of a novel: "I would love to make a film. I already have a project in my mind and even a new idea for cinematographic technique. Namely: the development of an image from a frame of one tenth of a second (imperceptible at first) to an extended scene (figée). It is a technique that I want to use in a novel as well, perhaps in the so-called peasant novel. Ultimately, it is an idea I have also used in *Zenon* (see the scene of the 'slaughtering of the pig')" (220–221).

a narrative telescope by a supra- or infra-textual authority that is to an extent occult. It is an authority that "knows" more about novelistic strategies than, let us say, any of the narrators subordinate to him, than the young man perpetually on his way to the station, for example. Such a narrative and cinematic *eye*, superimposed on the whirlpool of the text, can grasp how the film of the novel is being made step by step. He has the privilege of being able to see how "l'éclat des projecteurs s'accrut" above the characters and fasten them, sometimes arbitrarily, in the "insectarium" of his gaze. Hence the almost didactic formulations and exemplifications in relation to the supposed reader/audience outside the fictional tableau, as in the following example: "*For a remote observer*—for example, that young man hurrying along . . ." (emphasis added). The all-encompassing, non-anthropomorphic, seemingly otherworldly, eyeglass in *Vain Art of the Fugue* lends the text a void specularity, lacking in any referent.

*

A similar perspective, whereby textual focus is achieved, reoccurs formulated in the image/metaphor of the *blank screen* in *Novel for Reading on the Train*. At a given moment, the director character "forgets to turn off the now blank screen." This is a mise en abyme of the poetics of the scenario novel, of its deceptive transparency, that of a mirror voided of any mirroring referential substance. The book transforms itself into that screen whose specularity in itself counts, as a Sisyphean process, as a mechanism that spins without meshing, separate from the human object or subject reflected. The blankness of the screen, the superposition of cinematic frames within one and the same frame, and the spinning of the imaginary figures are all strategies of textual self-mirroring. By the very same obsessive self-mirroring movement, however, the text liberates itself, for an instant, from its own gravity, from its materiality, and becomes transparent, hieratic, musical.

The final apotheosis marks precisely the sublimation of textuality (together with its cultural, inevitably inter-textual unconscious, burdened with all kinds of guilt and traumas) into musicality. Littered with sadistic imaginary scenarios, brimming with pathological violence, the viscous textuality of the final sequence in *Vain Art of the Fugue* ultimately evaporates into "the sounds of the flute that continue without interruption, the same melody played over and over again *da capo*, with such conviction that the driver's raised arm freezes and the women too remain still, while little drops of blood, in time with the flute, drip down from the knife blade." It is a melody that induces magic and stops the supposed executioner (the driver) in his tracks: ". . . the driver's raised arm freezes and the women too remain still, while little drops of blood, in time with the flute, drip down from the knife blade." The *miraculous* scene is now different in nature than the surrealist category of the same name theorized by André Breton. *Le merveilleux* designates for Breton a characteristic of the content of imaginary phantasms, which lays claim also to the Gothic novel, for example. On the other hand, in Tsepeneag, the *miraculous* relates not so much to the imaginary content properly speaking of the pseudo-plot as much as to the revelation of the *fault line* that is created, ad hoc, between the already fissured, ambiguously delimited space of the fiction and the interstice of textuality as an autonomous medium. To be more exact, the miraculous is, in the final scene of *Vain Art of the Fugue*, not so much the hijacking of the driver's violent act under the influence of music as much as the halting of the character qua *character* in his tracks, of the up until then unpredictable fictional movement, the breaking down of the wall of the fiction so that it can be viewed—and listened to—from outside itself. The protagonist sees himself with the blood-spattered knife in his hand, he freezes, wholly unexpectedly, as if by miracle, he checks his sadistic impulse in order to listen to the music, one and the same with the text that has become purely a melodic line.

Textuality, having evaporated into musicality, is the matrix that has given birth to the character, together with his world, but the same textuality can also be twisted like a Möbius strip. The fictional world that can sometimes be glimpsed in its folds reveals itself to be merely an effect of its flexibility. Once it perceives the textual music that has generated it, the paper creature enters, as if through a "wormhole," hyperspace, where its motion acquires another, impenetrable dimension.

RE-INSCRIPTION AND THE ENDLESS TEXT

The cosmogony of the text and the myth of identity: The Necessary Marriage • Sensory textuality—the corporeality of the writing subject • The mental execution of the text—visualizing readings • The objectivity of the narrative gaze • The catoptrical play of the mirrors of the "I" • Narrative and phantasmic spirals

In the textualist novel *Pigeon Post,* there is an "ars poetica" sentence in which one of the narrative voices, whether the authorial voice or that of his double, whose name appears on the book's cover, the anagrammatic and pseudonymous Ed Pastenague, confesses to a consuming nostalgia. It is a nostalgia for the Absolute Book, the foundational, archetypal Book, whose text might end at any moment, because the perfection of the whole can be discovered and is mirrored in any of its points: ". . . to write a book that might end at any given point without missing anything essential, without the interruption lending it an unfinished aspect." Likewise, Eugène Ionesco formulated the paradoxical formula according to which a play should either "be able to end anywhere, like one cuts a ribbon" or go on infinitely, because, fundamentally, "any ending is arbitrary." For Ionesco, *continuous theater* would be the aesthetic consequence of an apocalyptic scenario, or to be more precise an effect of the apocalyptic unfolding of History. The play thus becomes a cavalcade of catastrophes, a *slaughter game* of the universal, over-determined directorial will:

> In reality, there are no reasons for a play to end. It should end anywhere, like one cuts a ribbon . . . The end will no longer be arbitrary when we are dead. Death concludes a life, a play, a work. Otherwise, there is no end. To find an end means to simplify the theatrical art, and so I understand why Molière never knew how to conclude. If an end is necessary, it is because the audience has to go to bed.[96]

If the finale of the play can intervene virtually anywhere, then the *endlessness* of the theatrical flow in fact presupposes the writing and staging of a dramatic text woven from a series of potential *endings*.

Dumitru Tsepeneag's books form such a text without end, a text made up of repeated, successive endings ad infinitum. *The Necessary Marriage, The Sandglass Word, Novel for Reading on the Train,* and *Pont des Arts* are *re-inscriptions* of preexisting cultural myths or of the author's own texts, "obsessive metaphors" and "personal myths" (in the sense of Charles Mauron's psycho criticism). This author who enters the fictional stage as a protagonist-ghost experiences a drama comparable to that found in Pirandello's

96 Claude Bonnefoy, *Entretiens avec Eugène Ionesco* (Paris: Éditions Pierre Belfond, 1966), 95.

theater, attempting to make himself felt as a character whose rights are at least equal to those of the other fictional characters proper. His "drama" revolves around the tribulations of writing, as well as, in parallel, those arising from love and a temporary lack of or surplus of inspiration, whether erotic or authorial. Because of his capricious, narcissistic personality, his numerous idiosyncrasies, *mofturi,* and anxieties linked to creativity, the writer character almost overwhelms the parts played by the other characters. And in his turn he suspects that he is already "written," that an occult Other has thus taken possession of him. "It's anyone's guess who pulls the strings behind the scenes!" This emblematic exclamation in *Hotel Europa* reveals precisely this ironic/melancholic suspicion, on the part of the author character. It is a dual attitude, half rebellious, half resigned, towards a potential *other world* behind the "set," beyond the frail pellicle of visible reality; but also towards a suspected conspiracy on the part of another Author, the possessor of genuine demiurgic power.

The cosmogony of the text thus unfolds firstly along the vertical, along the transcendental axis or *spiral* that ascends from the humble earthly creator to his angelic intermediary (the latter being the author character in many of Tsepeneag's short stories) and, finally, to the primordial, the divine. But the cosmogonic flow of the text also takes place along the horizontal of the "crawling," snaking text of immanent discursivity, void of any transcendental reference point. For the latter, the viscous, heavy textuality burdened by an imaginary, highly material zoomorphic to be found in *The Necessary Marriage* seems to be representative. The character Ciobanu languishes for the greater part of his time in a gastropod-like posture, oscillating between dream and waking. And the text itself, not accidentally lacking in any punctuation, seemingly laves the protagonist's body in a continuous discourse, which "crawls" with invertebrate slowness, leaving in its wake a trail like that of a slug:

> unable to sleep he tosses from side to side or on his stomach with one knee bent and pillow over his eyes then abruptly rolls over next to the wall that smells of damp and mice everywhere mice and slugs that get it into their heads to stroll around the room at night it's theirs too after all he simply can't drop off can't manage to get through into sleep to pull away the black wall-curtain dotted with a thousand holes and venules of light a green or blue light proof that it's only a curtain he must open to escape the reek of mice and the damp of mouse piss . . .

The protagonist "slides" away and almost sheds his human form, but his textualist thoughts also slide away, decompose, incapable, it seems, of regaining the syllogistic stringency of Cartesian argumentation. On the contrary, his inner maieutics abandons any ideatic rigor, becoming a mental performance projected at a sensory level, or the visual and aural, to be more precise:

> he no longer hears anything but that buzzing inside sometimes louder than the noises outside he closes his eyelids tighter and stops breathing the buzzing grows more intense a yellow-green expanse looking like a plain or

> perhaps the calm surface of a pond covered with crow-silk he now hears the beating of his heart feels he is choking the pond disappears the curtain falls blacker than before

His invertebrate movements, his larval physical and psychical state, within a kind of eternal non-existence, evoke Beckett's pseudo-heroes, such as Molloy, Murphy, Malone, Watt, or Winnie. Whereas Winnie in *Happy Days* lives almost buried in a mound of earth, the teacher Ciobanu in Dumitru Tsepeneag's novel lives in an almost fetal state, in the "womb" of his bed and moldering room. The bewildered state of the main character in *The Necessary Marriage*, symptomatic of his ataractic *waiting* within a claustrophobic womb-like space, situates him in the line of those often amorphous, mutilated sub-beings from a perhaps post-apocalyptic time that haunt the plays and prose of Samuel Beckett.

*

What is paradoxical, in the context of a deliberately experimental narrative format, one of ostentatious stylistic decadence, is the intertextual reverence—albeit parodic—that Tsepeneag's novel pays to two works of national "heritage." *The Necessary Marriage* contains, as critics have pointed out, a double rewriting: of the ballad of *Miorița*, constitutive of the myth of Romanian national identity, and of Ion Barbu's poem "Ritmuri pentru nunțile necesare" ("Rhythms for the Necessary Marriage"), which in itself is a mise en abyme, a textual mirror, which rewrites *Miorița*. According to essayist Tudor Vianu, Ion Barbu's poem evokes the soul's progress through three cosmic stages before reaching the apotheosis of "spiritual perfection." As in the cosmology of Plotinus, in Barbu's poem the soul is wedded to the One, to its originary Idea, and is mirrored in the three "circles of the mystery" of successive initiation: "The wheel of Venus / Of the heart / The wheel of the head / Of Mercury / In liquefaction, in azure, / The wheel of the Sun / Of the Great One." From Ion Barbu, Tsepeneag adopts the scenario of the wedding in three different times. In *The Necessary Marriage*, the three female figures are Ileana, Ana, and Anica the schoolgirl, the latter taking on the role played by Mioara in the ballad. The imagery drawn from the work of Ion Barbu is also easily identifiable in the half-oneiric appearance of the slimy slugs on the walls, which are as many materialized erotic phantasms, as if having emerged from "the chasm Uvedenrode," the matrix of "supra-sexual, supra-musical" gastropods in the poem "Uvedenrode." The signs of the Mioritic palimpsest can also be detected at every step: the protagonist, "the groom," is none other than Ciobanu (Shepherd), and two of his colleagues, the country schoolteachers Munteanu (Highlander) and Pădureanu (Forester), machinate against him, denouncing him to the school's inspectorate. From the Mioritic mythological frame are lacking only the flocks of sheep descending into the valley, the sacrificed lamb, the *mountaintop*, which is sometimes confused with the sea, with the colors of the national tricolor. The talking sheep Mioara becomes in *The Necessary Marriage*, the same as in the national ballad, a tender confessor, complicit in the scenario of the cosmic wedding.

The re-mythologization of the Mioritic mythemes, through their infusion with lyricism and a sprinkling of candid humor, sometimes seems as canonical as can be, lacking in any parodic irreverence:

> you don't have a mother she probably says that's right he answers but maybe he misunderstood it'll be like a party he explains to her patiently like a wedding you see yes a wedding the moon and the sun will appear together in the sky and thousands of torches will light up at the ends of the earth herds of mist will float up the hills and sheep bells and trumpets will sound the fir trees will bend to the ground and all the forests will rustle it'll be a magnificent wedding the ewe listened with its mouth wide open maybe it had even fallen asleep

On the other hand, genuine, apparently sacrilegious irreverence toward the mythological and sacral meanings of *Miorița* itself can be found in the insistent invocation of the sheep as an erotic object, its perverse fetishization:

> it's pretty dirty she says it needs to be spruced up look how clean the other one is yes and we'll put ribbons on her someone adds anyway the idea of washing the ewe wins everyone over the soldier suddenly wakes from his drunken stupor and offers his services but the shepherds won't hear of it she's their sheep after all even if they agree that she should be washed and given the full bridal treatment and they nudge each other and laugh softly . . .

> what are you doing there he's fucking sir Munteanu says in his shepherd's disguise fucking the sheep don't you realize it's a wedding here not a brothel the Inspector growls . . .

Critic Edgar Reichmann remarks in the novel precisely this coexistence of scenes imbued with strong sensuality, and even explicit, unveiled sexuality, with symbols of spiritual redemption, achieved through the cosmic, metaphysical wedding.[97] Beyond the level of intertextual mythologic themes, as well as that of the topographic imagery (images of *hill/vale* or the mountain plateau undulating like the waves of the sea), the Mioritic matrix can also be glimpsed in *The Necessary Marriage* in the "transhumance" of the textual flow. The movement of the textual magma is sometimes meandering, unfolding in successive, repetitive waves, sometimes circular, deepening in a spiral or concentric circles: "he is sleeping / a greenish yellow expanse like a plain the eyes were gradually becoming accustomed to the unusually strong light in fact a line of hills like calm expansive waves and flocks of sheep slowly moving across this space all of a sudden very close beneath his eyes beneath the soles of his feet and it was as if he had been running for a long time ascending and descending through the soft and dreadfully green grass he was panting he began to breathe

97 See his article, entitled "Tsepeneag et la mythologie danubienne," in *Le Monde*, no. 10167, October 7, 1977, 23, in which he praises the "implacable alternance d'une sensualité débridée et de symboles rédempteurs qui reviennent de façon obsédante." Moreover, Edgar Reichmann makes the natural comparison with the nouveau roman, but detecting a specific difference in *Les Noces nécessaires*: "Le livre est imprégné d'une chaleur secrète, rare dans la banquise du nouveau roman."

as deeply as he could he stopped he looked around him slightly bewildered . . ." Octavian Soviany detects even an *isomorphism* between "the act of coupling and the act of generating the text."[98] The obsessive *performance*, in the psychoanalytical sense, of Ciobanu's erotic fantasies with the sheep or with the schoolgirl Anica—the identities of the protagonists' sexual partners are interchangeable—triggers yet again a textual and imaginary vortex, as if in a mannerist *serpentine figure*:

> the ewe moaned gently beneath his weight he turned on his stomach and enfolded its soft body the sun was setting behind the hill slipping down ever redder ever
>
> why are you laughing I'm not laughing
>
> he buries his head between the woman's breasts she wraps her arm round his neck and smiles while squeezing as if to throttle him then heaves him on top of her and begins to stroke his shoulders back thighs testicles but all to no avail the man doesn't make the slightest move lies as if unconscious on the woman's fleshy body she

98 Octavian Soviany, "Nunțile necesare de Dumitru Țepeneag" (II), in *Contemporanul. Ideea europeană*, nos. 51–52, December 20–27, 2001, 4. The critic also argues for the inevitability of a kind of divorce—let us say one that is necessary—between the "symbolic space" and the meta-space of the self-conscious text, the former being unable to institute itself except through the parodic annihilation of the text: "Thus constituted on three horizons, 'the writing workshop' (which might be regarded as a metonymic representation of the writing subject), 'the symbolic space' and the textual universe, that of the scriptural carnival that ultimately turns into an unholy Sabbath, Dumitru Tsepeneag's book transforms itself into the story of an 'alchemical separation,' whose finality is the expurgation of the negative latencies of writing through hypertrophy and derision."

> finally tires and gives up the effort the lamb's head lies on the table with eyes and teeth intact the chestnut leaves rustle above at first . . .

The agonizing close-up of the lamb, in which the animal that symbolizes Christ becomes a foreboding image of apocalypse, as it does later in *Novel for Reading on the Train*, undermines the nuptials and loads them with thanatic allusions.

However, the skull of the lamb is merely one of the bizarre and nightmarish images—à la Buñuel—whose accumulation causes the Mioritic wedding feast to undergo a progressive demythologization. The culminating, faux-apotheotic sequence of the group photograph, with wedding guests in shepherd's costume and the sheep garnished with ribbons, also deconstructs the mythological content of the nuptials. Elsewhere a director within the text, a manipulator of the other characters and the entire narrative film (the writing in *The Necessary Marriage* has, like that of *Novel for Reading on the Train*, the technical and cinematic virtues of a film scenario), the character named the Inspector finally changes his identity. He becomes nothing more than a nondescript passerby, uninvolved in the nuptial scenario, a presumably uninformed reader.

The perspective that this meta-character whose identity remains mysterious has on the marriage, which he views in a detached way, from outside the narrative "tableau," from beyond the frame of the fiction, empties the event of its ritual substance. Parodied throughout the text in the nightmarish visions of copulation and in the grotesque allusion to pathological acts of zoophilia, the

Mioritic wedding is now transformed into nothing more than a photograph. The principal mytheme and the narrative nucleus end up being merely a pretext for the formulation of suppositions about the inner mood of the characters and value judgments about the novelistic discourse:

> the Inspector speaks calmly to everyone shows them their place attends to the tiniest detail then walks backwards to be at a greater distance from the camera he's now just another man a tall one to be sure but not much different from any passerby he stops at the edge of the sidewalk half raises an arm to work out the required level squints his eyes attentively approaches the display window once more the photograph blown up to the size of a painting and framed so that it can be hung on the wall nods his head stops takes another step gives another nod and you can't tell from his face or gestures which express only the kind of intense concentration necessary to formulate a value judgment you have no idea whether he likes the baroque composition heavy with obscure meanings or on the contrary is unpleasantly surprised by it he takes another step forward draws even closer and finally or so you assume notices what is necessary and essential to notice at a wedding namely that the groom really is happy.

From being a fictional fiction of no great consistency, sooner a textual puppet, the Inspector is elevated to a privileged viewpoint. He gazes down as if through a narrative telescope on the Mioritic scenario and, from this vantage point, he gains a panoramic view of the text below and is even able to pass critical verdicts. Like the young man running towards the station in *Vain Art of the Fugue*, the Inspector finds himself in a quixotic position, one that is both inside and outside the scene of the fiction.

It is in a similar position that the characters in *The Sandglass Word* find themselves, one of astonished hesitation at having escaped from their vital space, that of the book, into the agora of the extra-textual world:[99] "for an instant all the characters hesitate. even the soldier who is running by the railway track in his under vest stopped for a moment and looked up at the sky hesitantly. but now he has set off running once more. George fills a bottle with plum brandy. the child comes descends the stairs to the cellar with the goat. Mr. Robert is walking around the living room. the others resume their conversation." The narrator's drama of affective and cultural self-exile, of his passage from the linguistic matrix of Romanian to French, his adopted language, is debated by these characters with theoretical proclivities. The protagonist, a reflection of the author, signaled discursively by the first person singular, confesses to them his intention to rid himself of the "ballast" of Romanian phantasms, to exorcise the primordial cultural residue

99 *Le Mot sablier*, Paris, Éditions P.O.L, 1984. The text of this edition is entirely in French, with the passages in Romanian having been translated by Alain Paruit. A novel of linguistic "exile," of the draining of the textual sandglass from Romanian into French, it was written in 1978, i.e. three years after Tsepeneag became stateless. In 1975, Tsepeneag was expelled from the Romanian Writers Union and stripped of his Romanian citizenship by presidential decree. The original bilingual version of the novel, with the title *Cuvîntul nisiparniță* was published by Editura Univers, Bucharest, in 1994. A second edition, with an afterword by Georgiana Lungu Badea, was published in Timișoara by Editura Universității de Vest, in 2005.

of his unconscious, in order to be able to write uninhibitedly in French: "it is therefore appropriate to explain to the reader that I couldn't just recklessly venture into a writing whose materiality consisted of a language to which I had come quite late (albeit not too late) and, what is more, dragging behind me all kinds of apparitions: an entire theater of phantasms or, to put it more aptly, the storeroom of that theater." The polemical replies of the various interlocutors come only subsequently, after other phantasmic curlicues of the text: "the argument with the phantasms doesn't work says a character who up until then had not made much of an impact on the discussion and the gentleman with the pipe hastens to say that he is right." The parody of a maieutic dialogue that the characters conduct at one point on the subject of the need for or, contrariwise, the arbitrariness of punctuation is accentuated by the presence in counterpoint of non-theoretical, apparently fictional lines. These belong to the hastily-cobbled-together pseudo-epic scenario that is interwoven with that of the meta-text. The two different levels of fictionality in the book are inverted, each paradoxically highlighting the other. Their alternation is also pointed to at every step, in *The Sandglass Word*, by means of the double-spacing of the lines, which presupposes a different type of mental *execution* of the text, one that is more acute, as in the case of the inner projection of an entire mise-en-scène. Consequently, the text wagers on the heightened interaction of a visualizing reading, as in a theater script or a musical score:

> with regard to punctuation or to be more precise lack of punctuation in certain so-called modern texts (the pipe

helps him to make the required oratorical pauses: he can even trace brackets with it in the air) we ought to make a very serious reckoning. it can disorient the reader. and if we were to draw a conclusion from this

but you admit that obligatory capital letters after every full stop are also a form of tyranny. a tyranny of reading

imposed by the author

the woman who is serving the tea is wearing a flowery orange apron and seems jolly. no one pays any attention to her

I first of all ask the author who dictates to the reader where to stop: at a full stop count to three. at a comma say one

and at a semi-colon

and at a colon

all turn their eyes to the woman who is pouring the tea. but she had not said anything thc poor thing

they are eating the olives in reverse order of how manky they are

> they stop to catch their breath and gaze at a border-guard's watchtower. he's gawping through his binoculars again. at the sea. dusk has finally fallen: a swath of reddish-yellow light still lingers on the horizon. it's no longer raining
>
> let monsieur l'Auteur stop where he feels like it the possessor among other things of the orthographic truth
>
> doesn't like smoked herrings. or their smell
>
> but the tyranny (in the end) on the part of the reader shaped in the image and likeness of the author. the reader wants commas. he can't read if he doesn't see commas: full stops alone aren't enough for him

The curse of having to accept, with bitter textualist pedantry,[100] that everything has already been written—"how can you not wonder whether whatever we do we are not somehow condemned to toil all our lives on one and the same interminable palimpsest"—brings into discussion an aesthetic/philosophical thesis specific to the postmodern era: the death of literature. The apocalypse of

100 The Romanian critic Ion Simuţ regards *Le Mot sablier* as "the most important and noteworthy textualist experiment in Romanian literature," which reveals "textualism at work, with an objective beyond textualism itself as its technique" (*Clepsidra răsturnată* [*The Upturned Sandglass*], 132); see also Jean-Pierre Longre, "Passage de frontière et exil linguistique. Réflexions sur Le mot sablier de Dumitru Tsepeneag," in *Lettres et cultures de langue française*, no. 24, 1999, 69–76; Margareta Gyurcsik, "Une contribution roumaine au nouveau roman," in the volume *La Roumanie et la francophonie* (Timişoara: Anthropos, 2000), 142–156.

this art form was signaled as early as E. M. Cioran's pessimistic and cynical motto: "Que la littérature soit appelée à périr, c'est possible et même souhaitable." The eschatological vision of literature seems at other times to be contradicted by precisely what worn-out writing proves capable of nonetheless bringing to light *au fur et à mesure*. Namely, a number of hard nuclei within a mushy imagery reeking of copious materiality. Such a nucleus of imagery, whose purpose is to generate texts and phantasms, is the figure of the giant serpent, a dragon with seven or twelve heads, on top of which an entire city has been built. Waiting to take its revenge, just as literature itself is waiting to reclaim its lost rights, the phantasm of the dragon functions as a mirror of the textual sandglass, a mechanism to produce texts: "important for me was that the entire city had been built on top of it burying it alive, and it had accepted it like a worm: it hadn't even said so much as a peep, or maybe they had killed it beforehand: with broadswords, with spears. back then guns didn't exist. but it wasn't possible for the dragon to go on living and waiting for its revenge: the moment it would come to the surface." After expositing the "theme," in the musical sense, the dramatized "variations" then intervene, through dialogue, with ludic addresses and replies, according to a carefully directed and graphically molded structure, as if through a two-way radio:

he's evil
who
the dragon underneath the city

The image of the gigantic serpent, of the dragon buried under the city, can be compared, as Romanian critic Octavian Soviany rightly observes, with "the suggestion of the primordial Text, of a text that constitutes the scriptic equivalent of the cosmic egg."[101] Likewise, the sketch of a film scenario in which some border guards are digging a ditch might metonymically codify the descent into a pre-textual unconscious, therefore a return to the degree zero of writing, as a privileged Adamic state. The leitmotif of the strange erotic billing and cooing between the character Domnica and a miraculous cockerel with almost human affective reactions can also be interpreted as an act of not exactly canonical coupling between the seemingly female body of textuality, with all its phonetic and orthographic avatars, and the semantic and imaginary content that inseminates it: "Domnica is lying naked on the bed and the cockerel is standing on her belly, now and then pecking her, slightly embarrassed by the situation he finds himself in." The self-mirroring, along the lines of Gide, of this continuous textual performance is reflected in an *echoing structure* of not only semantic but also phonetic generators. The exemplary image of the sandglass symbolically sums up the whole of the bilingual book like an enormous self-representational hieroglyph, like a spiral twisting around its own archetypal axis (the image will also recur, according to the same principle of the textual and phantasmic spiral, in *Pigeon Post*). Alain, or Alene, the character who fictionalizes Tsepeneag's

101 Octavian Soviany, "Non-conformistul Dumitru Ţepeneag" [Dumitru Tsepeneag the Non-Conformist], in *Contemporanul. Ideea europeană*, no. 36, September 5, 2002, 4–5.

friend and French translator, Alain Paruit (just as the character Paul, rendered Pol in Romanian, is a reflection of editor Paul Otchakovsky-Laurens of Éditions P.O.L), falls to thinking while reading about the "sablier" structure of the text, wondering what the most appropriate term would be in Romanian:

> Alain ne répondra pas. Il attendra que les voix se taisent pour reprendre la lecture: 'Donc la figure du livre est le sablier. Ce qui exigerait une structure en écho: c'est-à-dire retrouver tous les grains de sable (thèmes, éléments épiques, personnages, etc.) qui s'écoulent doucement du vase supérieur dans le vase inférieur.' Ştii că habar n-am cum se zice sablier pe româneşte; poate nisiparniţă?! [You know, I've got no idea how to say sablier in Romanian; maybe nisiparniţă!].

Such hesitations on the part of the characters between two linguistic registers, Romanian and French, become increasingly sparser and toward the end French becomes omnipresent.

Alienated from his former linguistic and cultural identity, the first-person voice that makes and unmakes the text appears more and more exasperated by his thankless authorial position, faced with the arbitrary decision to formulate an apparent finale for the perpetual draining of words through the sandglass: "moi, j'en ai assez! Mais je ne sais pas comment finir, où mettre le point final. Après quelle phrase. Après quel mot." The deliberately aleatory finale is an infinitesimal motionless motion, a vanishing point in the perspective of the eternal flow of textual sand. The protagonist, identical with the narrator, looks out of the window and *waits*, à la Beckett, "que le grand Guignol commence," his posture being also that of the character in the earlier novella "Waiting," as well as that of Ed Pastenague in *Pigeon Post* and, later, the novelist in *Hotel Europa, Pont des Arts,* and *Maramureș*. Except that this time the expected epiphany proves to be merely an evanescent affective projection, a fleeting image that arises, ad hoc, in the fugue of the textual flow and then vanishes just as quickly: "En attendant je fouille à nouveau dans mes paperasses: 'parlez-vous français' répète à voix basse le garde-côte et fixe ses jumelles sur l'horizon: un avion qui ressemble à un énorme oiseau orange mais passe trop vite et sort du champ." By contrast, the illusory character of the magical airplane-bird confirms the *archetypal*, supra-personal reality of the sandglass. Textual exile, objectified in the sandglass of words doomed to drain away, invariably swallows up the fragile identity of the "being of flesh."

Emerging from the field of observation in the fictionalized writer's journal that is *The Sandglass Word*, the ectoplasm of the airplane-bird recurs, to a certain extent naturally, in *Roman de gare*,[102] published in France the year after *Le Mot sablier*. The vision of an eagle gliding, as enormous as an airplane, as terrifying as a ferocious beast, as a monster (demon or vampire, as the various characters involved in making a film based on *Novel for Reading on the Train* describe it), is a phantasm that has nonchalantly overstepped the in any case apparent and always

102 *Roman de gare*, Paris, P.O.L, 1985. This novel with a self-parodying title was written directly in French. A Romanian adaptation, in fact a new original text, with the title *Roman de citit în tren* [*Novel for Reading on the Train*] was published in Jassy by Editura Institutul European in 1993.

relativized boundaries of a certain textual space. But the eagle (or parrot or toucan sometimes captive in a cage with gilded bars, with "patriotic" red, yellow, and blue feathers, as later, in the novel *La belle Roumaine*) also plays the role of a mechanism to trigger the cinematic and novelistic discourse, of a fulcrum for textual production. The novella "The Wait," on whose scenario the film in *Novel for Reading on the Train* is based, closes with the cathartic scene of an immense bird descending apocalyptically from the sky, covering the entire forest, the entire narrative universe. In any case, the leitmotif of the eagle is by no means the only narrative link with the imaginary, fictional worlds of other texts by Dumitru Tsepeneag. Narcissistic and at the same time self-deriding, the scene where the stationmaster, alternately a character and the director, makes faces in the mirror as he brushes his teeth can also be found in the matutinal ritual of the blasé director-character of *Hotel Europa*. Likewise, the film being made in *Novel for Reading on the Train* by the director-character is called *The Two Marys*, alluding to the nativity scenario in the much earlier triptych "A Staging," but also to the two generic, archetypal M's, Maria and Magda (suggesting the biblical Mary Magdalene) in *Vain Art of the Fugue*. Biblical-sounding names—Matthew, Mark, Luke, Thomas, Mary, Maria-Christina, "the Other Mary," Francis—otherwise abound. *Novel for Reading on the Train* is, in this respect, the same as "A Staging" before it, a parodic rewrite, albeit not one that is blasphemous, of Christ-like motifs and symbols. The scenario of the death and resurrection of Jesus now has at its center, as its redemptive, messianic figure, a *She*. After the bewildering announcement that "*she* is dead," there follows a passage marked, by no means accidentally, with italics. It contains the reinterpretation/retelling of the Gospels in a *gender studies* key, with a parodic feminist re-mythologization: "*An hour later, a nurse came up to him, her face flushed, panting, to inform him that Maria's body had vanished from the autopsy room.*"

With its protagonist named Maria, as well as her hieratic double, *the other Maria*, the film will subsequently be watched by the characters in *Hotel Europa*. One and the same film, a mise en abyme of the entire novel, it is the story of its own making. The often breathless rhythm, action-language or, rather *movement-language* confers upon the textual flow, the same as in *Vain Art of the Fugue* or in *The Sandglass Word*, the character of an ambivalent, theatrical and at the same time cinematic *performance*. A number of the director's imperative lines—"Forget about the meaning! It's all about atmosphere, about the general ambience, which is not always the same thing"—are in their turn relevant for the poetics of other texts, such as *Pigeon Post* or *Pont des Arts*. The discursive and phantasmic atmosphere is also prevalent over any particular referential meaning. The affective and typological doubling, the mannerist anamorphoses of character development, from the characters in *Exercises* to the Ana of *La belle Roumaine*, confirms Tsepeneag's profound, structural aesthetic. In *Novel for Reading on the Train*, this is formulated in the director's diatribe against realistic acting, followed by the invocation of Brechtian *distance*: "even though he doesn't adore Brecht, he declares that he prefers Stanislavsky . . ."

The distancing is achieved not only between an actor and his character or between a spectator within the text and a character, but also between the cinematic fiction, operating as a miniature mirror of the novel, and the "truth" of the novelistic convention it is framing. A reflection at the textual level of this defamiliarization can be glimpsed in the successively deconstructed and reconstructed polyphony of the voices and narrative perspectives. Also symptomatic is the play of first and third person: "The chief held the lamb in his arms to shield it from the frenzy of the revelers. Spattered with red wine, the animal is sleeping without a care." This is followed by a surprising lapse into the more empathetic voice of the narrative *I*: "To film a poor lamb perched on a table full of bottles and glasses—I must say I don't find any genius in something like that. They tied it up and anesthetized it. I've no idea what they did to it to stop it moving. Anyway, I didn't say anything to them. At one point, I held the lamb in my arms to shield it from the frenzy of those drunkards." Here, a palimpsest over a text by Caragiale can be reconstructed, the inter-textual reference being *Grand Hôtel "Victoria Română"* [*The Romanian Victory Grand Hotel*]. The affective and sensorial exasperation of the Caragiale-esque narrator confronted with the scene of the tortured dog and the prostitute is also to be found, alternately narrated by the *I* and the *he* voice, in *Novel for Reading on the Train*. Confronted with the Bacchic orgy in the tavern, these voices might well say, together with the first-person voice in Caragiale's text: "I feel enormously and I see monstrously," "I'm agitated; I cannot watch any more; but I can still listen," "I put my hands over my eyes and retreat." The hypertrophied desperation of the powerless onlooker becomes, as in *The Romanian Victory Grand Hotel*, unbearable, and is painted in thick, expressionist brushstrokes: "Maria was uncontrollable: without her blouse, without her bra, her skirt pulled down below her navel, she was whirling around, she was twisting in every direction, she was shaking her hips with a generosity intended to be oriental. I couldn't bear to watch them, neither her nor the others. I slipped out of sight. With the lamb. I wasn't feeling well and nor did I like the wine, that blood-red plonk."

On the one hand, the lamb, as a symbol of Christ, is the embodiment of a sacral phantasm of the self or the *double*. On the other hand, this non-human double suggests the hybridization of the textual voice of the ectoplasm-character, the ghostly presence of a quasi-diabolical, monstrous being within the text, of a nightmarish animal-man. The corpse of a lamb at one point spontaneously invokes an apocalyptic scenario. The novel is haunted by numerous such occult signs, premonitions of a *possible world*, a quasi-oneiric world populated by a bestiary of clawed, monstrous pseudo-people à la Swift. One mysterious sentence—"The singer's hand looks more like a claw"—suggests, for example, beyond the fine pellicle of the framing fiction, behind the *mirror/screen* of the film/text, the presence of a bizarre realm of hybrid, miraculous, half-anthropomorphic, half-zoomorphic beings. The eschatological image of the field littered with grotesque animal corpses and skeletons functions as a mirror of the traumatized, split, self-distanced interior of the viewing and/or filming subject. The animal figures are now not so much symbols as much as states, *stases* of textual assembly. Or else mirrors of the "I," which designate this *I*, through the multiplication of its refracted images; as many *roles* of the "I," conferred upon it through the adoption of oneiric "legislation," or, to be more precise, through adherence to the "law" of ubiquity specific to the dream.

*

Ultimately, the catoptric play of the reflection of multiple phantasmic *I's* within one another is one of the main strategies for creating the textual *spiral* in the prose of Dumitru Tsepeneag. *Pigeon vole*, a text based on this same principle of the potentially endless narrative spiral (like the plays of Ionesco), bears the signature of the author's quasi-fictional double, Ed Pastenague, and is then translated into Romanian, with the title *Porumbelul zboară! . . .* , by none other than D. Țepeneag. In his turn, Ed Pastenague finds himself forced to resort, in order to write his novel, to another three Eds: the "black" Edmond (from Martinique), the "yellow" Edgar (from Vietnam) and the "red" Edouard (a white Frenchman, who is a "comrade," a left-winger). The three, former colleagues at the lycée in Agen, friends of Pastenague, function as his narrative and phantasmic hypostases, whom the narrator asks to fill in a questionnaire, aimed at managing and adjusting their texts. Finally, there is the anonymous third-person character, the chess-player, also named "the master" or "the old man," who openly borrows many of his biographical data from Tsepeneag himself. For example, he carries with him a book on chess theory, *La défense Alekhine*, published by Dumitru Tsepeneag with Éditions Garnier in 1983.

The various masks of the writing "I" also originate from a miraculous intermediate realm, one that is partly zoomorphic, partly anthropomorphic, or rather anamorphic, with mannerist and oneiric features. From the very first pages, the character of the prose writer is likened to nothing less than a fish: "They used to taunt me, shouting: Stingray-head! Stingray-head!" The self-mirroring nature of the text is evident. The words refer, circularly, to the meaning of the French regional dialect word "Pastenague," the homonym of Tsepeneag's anagram. Critic Nicolae Bârna has decrypted in detail the "spiky," insulting connotation of *Pastenague*, referring to the etymology of the name for this kind of fish, with a spike at the tip of its tail.[103] In fact, fish also appear in Tsepeneag's early short stories ("Amintire" [Recollection] and "Peşte mort" [Dead Fish]), as an oneiric double of the "I," alongside the dove ("Porumbela").

The depersonalization of the being who writes occurs more than once in *Pigeon Post*. The storyteller is objectified in the somewhat autonomous, detached *gaze* that seemingly transports him outside the sphere of the human, projecting him, for example, into a contemplated ornithological fauna:

> The pigeons, if you examine them closely with binoculars: there, that one's stopped moving, perching motionless, a big one, or fat, or maybe just puffing up in the sun, contented, leaving me time to observe the blue grooves in the wings, the white collar with tiny orange grains, and the purplish skin of its feet. A gray pigeon is never really

103 Nicolae Bârna, *Ţepeneag. Introducere într-o lume de hîrtie* [*Introduction to a World of Paper*], 201: "It turned out, however, that 'Pastenague'—which is no more familiar to the average Frenchman than the 'impossible,' exotic, spiky 'Tsepeneag'—is a dialect word which denotes a kind of fish, a kind of 'raie' ('ray'). 'Raie' was approximated ad hoc (and erroneously) by Romanian lexicographers less than devoted to ichthyology as 'calcan' ('plaice' or 'turbot'), whereas in fact it is a kind of stingray (Trygon pastinaca), related to the shark and armed with a barbed tail: thus Tsepeneag's 'ţeapa' ['spine' or 'goad,' but also, idiomatically, a 'confidence trick'—Trans.] can be recouped, circuitously, in his French pseudonym."

> gray; there's a fact to put in quotation marks, as if to suggest that one day it will be well known. What matters is how sharp your vision is . . .

Far from acquiring any referential veracity, the apparently pedantic description obsessively hypertrophies the details until they become hallucinatory. The fluctuating presence of white doves on the black branches seems a phantasmic transfiguration of a rough draft that is endlessly erased and rewritten:

> *White doves on black branches.* That's what I should have written, without fretting about oversimplification, which is inevitable in any case.
>
> All right, I'll start over. So, here we go, with a vigorous double stroke in the form of an X. Don't you just love a fine-looking rough draft?

This rough-draft writing, which incorporated "everything," like the capacious belly of a whale ("I keep everything, down to the last doodle. Later on, I'll decide what to get rid of, for the sake of efficiency"), is finally liberated from the burden of any meaning transcendent to it. The writing can, on the other hand, highlight its own materiality. The discontinuous textuality—"disjointedness triumphant, rising Christ-like from the dead!"—marked by destructuring cuts or crossings-out, even allows the intercalation of drawings in the text, which come to compensate for the epic crises of inspiration. In a kind of imaginary maieutic dialogue carried on with the three apprentices in the craft of writing or with eventual readers, the narrator confesses his dilemmas with regard to the novel's structure, conferring upon it a deliberately naïve pictorialness. The text of the novel increasingly resembles a scenographic sketch, with ostentatious blank spaces, draped with hieroglyphic icons, with allegorical mini-paintings. It ends up provoking a visual rather than conceptual mental *execution*:

> . . . promising the moon and the stars in this *nouvelle cuisine* lingo is not the best tack for attacking a text. What to do?
>
> I'm adding little drawings, an imp riding a turtledove, a sunflower, a parasol, a carrot that looks like a dog penis, a stingray.
>
> Start over?

The frequent questions (of the type, "What exactly was I thinking?" or "I'm piecing together a puzzle that doesn't exist" or "Have you ever raised carrier pigeons?" or "If I were writing a novel, what, in your view, would be the subject, the title and the narrative structure?") addressed to the virtual co-authors, the three Eds, also imprint the text with a theatrical, *performance* dynamism. A performance in which the novelistic, quasi-theatrical writing gives shape to a scenographic writing, to the "lighting and sound effects" of the narrative voices.

The textual sandglass—a didactic project *à rebours* • Bovarism and narrative "bouvardism" • Literary eschatology • The poetics of the fragment • The theatricalization of the masks of the "I" • Alterity, cultural hybridity, bilingualism

The much-invoked "solitude" of the narrator of *Pigeon Post* brings with it a solitude of the text in relation to its extra-textual context, to its possible referents, and hence also a self-referential mirroring of the text. The text borrows something from the hieratic and asemantic nature of music. The same as previously in the poetic *The Necessary Marriage* or in *The Sandglass Word*, the textual flow is rhythmically arranged and thereby acquires a musicality of its own, through the spacing of the paragraphs:

> Twin function of solitude: rest and shelter.
>
> Life without solitude is a deafening din. Solitude punctuates our life, makes it a little more musical, restores us to ourselves.

I've always dreamt of a writing workshop modeled on that of the painter's atelier of olden times: with helpers and apprentices in charge of preparing the paints, sometimes allowed to work on details, on small descriptions that the master has merely sketched out. For example, Madame Maryse leaving the house with her dog Valor, or Valérie . . .

> Who decides as to the race or sex of the story's apparently irrelevant Pekingese, who gets the last word?
>
> — What if we made it a basset hound? the apprentice asked.
>
> — Or castrated it? joked another helper.
>
> — Cut the clowning and follow the instructions . . . Please.
>
> My voice would be harsh, almost brittle, but deep down, I'd admit that it's not easy to manage such a workshop.

The idea of the writing workshop, combined with a literary theory circle, as in *The Sandglass Word*, seems to have arisen from a "didactic project," in which the first pages would make up "a kind of preface, a forward, let's say, to the kind readers who scan the page wisely, suspiciously, no, attentively, insightfully, humph, radiantly, hmm, hypocritically, or rather, superficially, yes, dully" over the text. The didacticism, albeit transcribed *à rebours*, parodically, is signaled by the author's intention to copy, apparently conscientiously, the books of others, the same as Flaubert's Bouvard and Pécuchet once did. Thus, this writer-copyist suffering from *bouvardism* would erase at random the greater part of the text, in order to demonstrate that "no matter how hard one might try (an eraser in each hand!), something will always remain of a true masterpiece." On the trail of the same Flaubertian pseudo-heroes, the scriptor will even insert here and there words extracted from the *Robert* dictionary, in order to make the snatches of text that have escaped "with [their] essence intact" interact with each other. The "furious" title, smacking of the avant-garde, for this project, which Ed in the end abandons out of sheer "laziness," might be "*Gommez, dit-il, ou la Raie cannibale*," or, as Tsepeneag translates/rewrites it in Romanian, "*dați cu guma, spuse el, sau Calcanul canibal*" [Erase, he said, or, The Cannibal Stingray]. The imperative functions as a mise en abyme, which once again refers, by means of a twist in the spiral of the textual mirror, to the beginning of the novel, i.e. to the motto from Paul Valéry: "La pensée est une rature indéfinie." In order to accentuate the parodic "cannibal" deconstruction of his creative writing project, born of false didactic pretensions, the narrator does not hesitate to confess, almost cynically, to a kind of "denial" of paternity to his own literary creation:

> Quote: "I couldn't write a novel unless I had domestic help."
>
> Contempt? Spurning of literature?
>
> But it has to be said: in black and white . . .

The fantasies of power and possession—"I'd like to play with Blacks," claims the narrator elsewhere—entertained by the feudal *master* of writing, who leases out his writing or delegates it to his apprentices, to write his texts for him, reminds me of the aristocratic "idleness" of the cynical dandy in the words of Villiers de L'Isle-Adam: "Living? Let our servants do it for us." For Ed, the feudal overlord of the aestheticizing life, it is the "servants," disguised as conscientious apprentices, who must do his writing for him, for his greater glory. The writer's diary within the novel abundantly records such disconcerting "mofturi" on the part of the master, executioner or textual cannibal. Formulated sooner in a ludic, droll spirit, rather than one that is dramatic, these textualizing *mofturi* in fact conceal the attempted revenge of an outraged subjectivity. It desires *restitution* in the psychoanalytical sense, after having been cannibalized in its turn by the work or by the ungrateful, forgetful or merely superficial reader: ". . . readers don't like the author, or more precisely, they couldn't care less about him. They prefer the work. And anyway, how can you like this putative, distant entity?" The eschatological thesis of the death of the author—" There's a whiff of putrefaction about the writer, he's stinking up the place"—and of literature, which "will expire in such a cacophony, such a din, that we'll hardly notice," situates *Pigeon vole* in the natural lineage of the somewhat earlier *Le Mot sablier*.

Out of the same bilingual "sandglass," written a few years earlier, in the textualist novel of Ed Pastenague, there now returns the hybrid palimpsest in which the supposedly fictional dialogue is interwoven with lines from the diary and meta-literary passages. They are all structured in atypical strophes, in a kind of poem-like "riddle," which, in Sisyphean ways, infinitely searches for its own hermeneutic key:

> Maryse is crossing the street.

> Sleepless night. Even though I went to bed at the normal time after re-reading my dear K., as is my habit. I was asleep in no time, and after a little while, it was he who tickled me under the chin . . .
>
> A log book?
>
> This text mustn't look too much like a diary. A building site, perhaps, but . . .

The poetics of the novel, which analyses itself in a vicious circle of its own textuality, might be discovered in the power for semantic dissemination of a discursive *fragment* or shard, a metonymy and *launch pad* for the whole:

> Was I breeding carrier pigeons?
>
> How to justify fragmentary writing.
>
> I would like to compare the fragment to a slingshot, to a crossbow, to a canon. Or why not a rocket-launcher, while I'm at it! . . . Not only does it cast afar the meaning it carries, but it does so in several directions at once. Sprinkling as it spins . . .

The rhythm and vividness of the discursive mechanism are deftly maintained, even in the absence of any plot. Sentences imbued with a pure, hard textualism are constantly mixed together with others that are traditionally diegetic, written in the most solid spirit of the omniscient epic convention. Reflections of bitter textualist humor, of the kind, "The word pigeon does not bite, but it doesn't fly either," can coexist with theatrical, disturbing exclamations, which suggest a trepidatious, thriller-type secondary scenario: "'You're killing me!' cried a woman's voice."

In this provocative textual hybridity what is to be sought is at least one of the hermeneutic keys to the novel. Otherwise, the novelistic mechanism, interwoven with various fictional and meta-literary threads, is reduplicated, at a thematic level, by the cultural (and at the same time) racial *métissage* of the three Eds. In fact, the four Eds: Edmond, Edgar, Edouard, plus their "matrix," their master, the Franco-Romanian Ed Pastenague. The characters speculate, in a piquant, humorous dialogue, on the linguistic graftings of the French language ("Who owns the French language?" or "Does French belong to everyone?" as one of the apprentice writers asks), under the circumstances in which identity today means cultural hybridity. The discussions of the apprentices about ethno-psychology and the micro-politics of identity in the age of globalization, conducted in a simultaneously parodic and politically correct manner, come together to form a miniature, bouffe theatrical piece, not lacking in touches of philosophizing skepticism. It is as if the great-great-grandsons of the faux heroes of Ion Budai-Deleanu's *Ţiganiada* [*The Gitaniad*] are speaking, now converted, centuries later, into vigorous *moftangii*:

> — Our Gallic ancestors, said Edmund, didn't trouble themselves with this kind of problem: they spoke Latin their way.

— Which is to say badly . . .

— And which led to what is today's French . . .

— The future belongs to creoles! laughed Edward.

— You mean, to English, I interjected, with gravitas, or to be exact, what's leftover from the French of the Norman invasion, when they got the ill-advised notion to cross the Channel.

In *Pigeon vole / Porumbelul zboară! . . . / Pigeon Post*, the textual weave engulfs, in the end, the "Creole" identity of language. The drama of linguistic ambivalence in *Le Mot sablier / Cuvîntul nisiparniță / The Sandglass Word* is here metamorphosed into a drama of ontological hybridity and concretized in a theatricalization of the plurivalent ages and masks of the "I."

The narrator appears as a kind of textual supra-mask and at the same time as a theorist of his own textual intentionality. He declares himself to be "conscious of having to write here a kind of über-biography." Calling himself a "weaver," he ends up by discovering the overwhelming "endless tapestry" that includes not only him but also the other "weavers," themselves woven from uncontrollable, occult threads:

> . . . whatever he does, the threads will extend beyond the loom and beyond the workshop, they escape and tangle as they wander through life and the city, reaching other weavers (even less vigilant?) who are themselves overwhelmed by what they mistake for their own threads.

The trap, the textual *piège* that is laid for the scriptors, is set by a supra-personal will, by a supreme Weaver who, presumably, its playing a joke on his apprentices. The anguish of the apprentice who, having believed that he has mastered his own writing, begins to suspect he is a mere puppet in the hands of another brings with it the obsession with the double. A double that is sooner dictatorial, almost a harbinger of doom: "I've got the weirdest feeling, as if it weren't me who was, no . . . anyway . . . I feel like someone's looking over my shoulder. Worse, I feel spied upon, watched over like a schoolboy (by his father?). I'm acting at someone else's bidding. And I'm letting it happen, turning over the reins . . . I'm helpless to resist." The projected presence of the Other relates here to a kind of Kafkaesque complex of the Father, fantasized as an evil Demiurge, in the Gnostic sense.

Elsewhere, however, the double comes into being thanks to the heart-rending nostalgia for a *He* to save the *I*, for a paternal, protective *peer* to protect anguished subjectivity. In the encounter with the mysterious middle-aged man, who carries under his arm *The Harlequin's Defense*, Ed falls prey to almost adolescent feelings, which find somatic expression in an unexpected quickening of his heartbeat: "if it really was the first time I'd ever seen this stranger, why the devil was my heart fluttering so?" The mutual recognition of the narrator and this Other of the self does not occur all at once ("no, there's no way: had we already met before? But where?"). Moreover, the unknown twin seems effectively to distance himself from the *I*, until he becomes a reified, even thanatic hypostasis of him. In the guise of a chess player dressed in mourning, solemn and pale, like a gravedigger, the double reveals himself to Ed as a phantom of foreboding, as a sign from the beyond.

The novel's ending repeats, in a deliberate simulacrum of a thriller-type scenario, the phantasmic figure of the chess player, seen from behind, as a hieratic/surreal silhouette, à la Magritte. Following him at a measured distance, the narrator realizes, to his stupefaction: "Wait a minute, he's going to my place!" Moreover, the Other is moving, autarchically, along a different existential orbit. This is why he does not seem to notice his imaginary twin who, lost in a different age of life, desperately interpolates him and tries to catch up with him, as if in a dream: "But he doesn't stay more than a minute, nor does he turn toward me as I approach him, with only a few meters between us now. As if I didn't exist . . ." Chasing itself, stalking itself ("Have I become nothing but a vampire?") in the labyrinth of its own text, the "I" senses the strange "tap-tapping" of a typewriter. The shame and even humiliation that it feels, that of being "erased" by a pencil eraser, abolished, prepares the "surprise" of the final solution to the mystery. Not only the chess player, the Other, "c'est moi," but also the typewriter writing in his place, and thus, in a sui generis spirit, it abolishes him: ". . . how to put it, after so much prevarication, failing to recognize him at the outset, in all simplicity, how can I help but transform this whole thing into a confession: the sound of the typewriter is coming from my room . . ."

The textualist trick, a kind of deus ex machina strategy, seems to have explained everything without exception. Then why, all the same, can it still be a matter of the "I" confessing its guilt? In other words, a sentiment that frees the subject from the textualist trap and highlights it in itself, with all its affective tribulations, whether psychoananalyzable or not, with all its scriptic, theoretical, pseudo-philosophical and erotic *mofturi*? The answer is perhaps not necessarily to be sought in the novel's ending. It is in any case a somewhat relative ending, given that the narrator has been constantly theorizing his own fear of the textual score coming to an end. A key—the Key?—to the mystery can be found in the possession of the old chess player. "The threat is stronger than the execution," he pedagogically pronounces before an audience of other, less experienced players. Then the player of a different, atemporal age asks the talented young boy, as if he were asking himself: "Do you know how to checkmate?" And he cedes to him his victory:

> "In that case you've won."
>
> And he extends his arm toward his redheaded opponent, who recoils to avoid the hand of the old player, which lands on my head instead, tousling my hair, touching my ear and lingering on my cheek. I feel a rush of heat and my heart is pounding. Like a dog melting at the loving stroke of his master, or a slave touched by some act of gratitude, of reward, or even, of forgiveness . . ."

As if hologrammatically, the consoling hand passes intact through and beyond ages of life and the discursive weave of the pages. The ineffable emotion generated by such an incredible touch rescues the textualism from itself, confers upon it being. For, one of the many, faux, temporal finales, like so many barely perceptible, infinitesimal pauses in the flight of the virtual pigeons, would be precisely this: the arm of the old player, of the "master," caresses in forgiveness the brow of its former "I," he touches the face of the child (his own face) redemptively, as if touching the young man in himself, continuously, in eternal recurrence.

Not only the almost autarchic identity of the textual (textualist) "I" is projected into an endless vertigo, by re-inscribing itself in a circle or spiral, but also the "national," "Mioritic" identity. The phantasmic *Romanianness* that Tsepeneag denounces, in the manner of Caragiale, as a *moft* in his *hopscotches* and diaries or which he castigates in the spirit of Cioran, receives complementary fictional embodiments: the teacher Ciobanu, in *The Necessary Marriage* (a successively de-mythologizing and re-mythologizing re-inscription of *Miorița*), and the fatal Ana/Hannah, in his recent imagological novel *La belle Roumaine*. Whereas as Ciobanu becomes to a certain extent hieratic, "eternal," immortalized, albeit parodically, in the photograph of the atemporal Mioritic wedding, Ana will, in one of the successive endings of the novel, be ritually slain. But the fictional and textual end of Ana, as well as that of Ciobanu, are equally relative. And the myths of identity, situated in a continual humorous "transhumation," are also repeatable, just as the temporal and phantasmic spiral of Dumitru Tsepeneag's novel continues to rotate.

BIBLIOGRAPHY OF PUBLISHED WORKS BY DUMITRU TSEPENEAG

SHORT PROSE

• *Exerciții* (*Exercises*), Bucharest, Editura pentru Literatură, 1966
• *Frig* (*Cold*), Bucharest, Editura pentru Literatură, 1967
• *Așteptare* (*The Wait*), Bucharest, Editura Cartea Românească, 1971; 2nd edition, Bucharest, Editura Cartea Românească, 1993
• *Exercices d'attente*, translated into French by Alain Paruit, Paris, Éditions Flammarion, 1972
• *Înscenare și alte texte* (*Staging and Other Texts*), Pitești, Editura Calende, 1992
• *Prin gaura cheii* (*Through the Keyhole*), with a preface, chronological table, notes, and selected criticism, edited by Nicolae Bârna, Bucharest, Editura Allfa, 2001
• *Attente*, translated into French by Alain Paruit, Paris, Editions P.O.L, 2003

NOVELS

• *Arpièges*, translated into French by Alain Paruit, Paris, Éditions Flammarion, 1973; original Romanian edition: *Zadarnică e arta fugii* (*Vain is the Art of the Fugue*), Bucharest, Editura Albatros, 1991; 2nd edition, Bucharest, Editura Art, 2007; translated into

Serbo-Croat by Petru Krdu, 2003; translated into Hungarian by Németi Rudolf, Budapest, Palamart, 2007; translated into English as *Vain Art of the Fugue*, by Patrick Camiller, Champaign, IL & London, Dalkey Archive Press, 2007; translated into Turkish by Leyla Ünal, Istanbul, Pupa Yayinlari, 2010

• *Les noces nécessaires*, translated into French by Alain Paruit, Paris, Éditions Flammarion, 1977; original Romanian version: *Nunțile necesare* (*The Necessary Marriages*), Bucharest, Editura Fundației Culturale Române, 1992; 2nd edition, Bucharest, Editura Ars Amatoria, 1992; 3rd edition, Bucharest, Editura All, 1998; 4th edition, Bucharest, Editura Art, 2008; English version, with the title *The Necessary Marriage*, translated by Patrick Camiller, Champaign, IL & London, Dalkey Archive Press, 2009

• *Le Mot sablier*, Paris, Éditions P.O.L, 1984; Romanian-French bilingual edition, with the title *Cuvîntul nisiparniță* (*The Sandglass Word*), Bucharest, Editura Univers, 1994; 2nd edition, Timişoara, Editura Universității de Vest, 2005

• *Roman de gare*, Paris, Éditions P.O.L, 1985 (French original); Romanian version, with the title *Roman de citit în tren* (*Novel for Reading on the Train*), Jassy, Institutul European, 1993

• *Pigeon vole*, Paris, Éditions P.O.L, 1989 (written in French, under the pseudonym Ed Pastenague); translated into Romanian by the author with the title *Porumbelul zboară!* (*Fly Pigeon!*), Bucharest, Editura Univers, 1997; English version, with the title *Pigeon Post*, translated by Jane Kuntz, Champaign, IL & London, Dalkey Archive Press, 2008

• *Hotel Europa*, Bucharest, Editura Albatros, 1996; 2nd edition, Bucharest, Editura Gramar, 1999; 3rd edition, Bucharest, Editura

Corint, 2006; French version, translated by Alain Paruit, Paris, Éditions P.O.L, 1996; German version, translated by Ernest Wichner, Berlin, Alexander Fest Verlag, 1998; Frankfurt am Main, Suhrkamp Verlag, 2000 (Taschenbuch); other translations: Hungarian, by Németi Rudolf, Budapest, Palamart, 2002; Slovenian, by Aleš Mustar, Ljubljana, Študentska založba, 2002; Czech, by Tomáš Vašut, Praha, Dybbuk, 2008; English version, with the title *Hotel Europa*, translated by Patrick Camiller, Champaign, IL & London, Dalkey Archive Press, 2010

• *Pont des Arts*, French translation by Alain Paruit, Paris, Éditions P.O.L, 1998; Romanian version, Bucharest, Editura Albatros, 1999; 2nd edition, Bucharest, Editura Corint, 2006

• *Au pays du Maramureş*, translated into French by Alain Paruit, Paris, Éditions P.O.L, 2001; Romanian version, with the title *Maramureş*, Cluj, Editura Dacia, 2001; 2nd edition, Bucharest, Editura Corint, 2006

• *La belle Roumaine*, Piteşti, Editura Paralela 45, 2004; 2nd revised edition, Bucharest, Editura Art, 2007; translated into French by Alain Paruit, Paris, Éditions P.O.L, 2006; Austrian edition, translated into German by Ingrid Baltag, Klagenfurt, Wieser Verlag, 2008; Portuguese version, *A Bela Romena*, translated by Isabel Fraga, Alfragide, Editora Oceanos, 2009; Bulgarian version, *Krasivana rumŭnka*, translated by Rumyana Stancheva, Sofia, Balkani, 2010; Turkish version, *Romen Dilberi*, translated by Leyla Ünal, Istanbul, Pupa Yayinlari, 2010

• *Camionul bulgar* (*The Bulgarian Truck*), Jassy, Editura Polirom, 2010

• *La Défense Alekhine*, Paris, Garnier, 1983

• *Un român la Paris. Pagini de jurnal* (*A Romanian in Paris. Diary Pages)*, Cluj, Editura Dacia, 1993; 2nd edition, Bucharest, Editura Cartea Românească, 1997; 3rd definitive edition, Bucharest, Editura Cartea Românească, 2006

• *Reîntoarcerea fiului la sînul mamei rătăcite* (*The Son's Return to the Bosom of the Errant Mother*), Jassy, Institutul European, 1993

• *Momentul oniric* (*The Oneiric Moment*), anthology edited by Corin Braga, Bucharest, Editura Cartea Românească, 1997 (including texts by Leonid Dimov)

• *Călătorie neizbutită* (*Unsuccessful Journey*), Bucharest, Editura Cartea Românească, 1998

• *Războiul literaturiii încă nu s-a încheiat* (*The Literature War is Not Yet Over*), interviews, Bucharest, Editura Allfa, 2000

• *Destin cu Popeşti. Şotroane* (*A Destiny with Popescus. Hopscotches*), Cluj, Editura Dacia & Biblioteca Apostrof, 2001

• *Clepsidra răsturnată* (*The Upturned Sandglass*). *Convorbiri cu Ion Simuț*, with *Addenda*, Piteşti, Editura Paralela 45, 2003

• *Capitalism de cumetrie* (*Nepotistic Capitalism*), Jassy, Editura Polirom, 2007

• *Frappes chirurgicales*, Paris, Éditions P.O.L, 2009

GLOSSARY OF ROMANIAN LITERARY TERMS, WORKS AND FIGURES

ALISTAIR IAN BLYTH

ALENE. In Romanian, "alene" is an adverb with the meaning "at ease," "nonchalantly," "in a leisurely manner," etc.

BARBU, Ion (1895–1961). Pen name of Dan Barbilian. Major Romanian modernist poet and also brilliant mathematician, for whom "Barbilian spaces" in geometry are named.

BĂNULESCU, Daniel (1961–). Romanian poet of the "Eighties Generation" and, since the Revolution, novelist. His novels include *Te pup în fund conducător iubit* [*I Kiss Your Ass, Beloved Leader*] (1994).

BLAGA, Lucian (1895–1961). Romanian poet, novelist, playwright, idealist philosopher, and diplomat. He was sacked from his university professorship in 1948 and banned from publishing his own work until the year before his death, in 1960. He was nominated for the Nobel Prize for Literature in 1956, but the Romanian communist government sent emissaries to Sweden to exert official pressure to thwart any decision in Blaga's favor. Blaga published eight volumes of poetry between 1919 and 1943, his early, expressionist manner later developing into a philosophical lyricism. His novel *Luntrea lui Charon* [*Charon's Bark*] was not published until after the fall of the communist regime, in 1990. Blaga's philosophical magnum opus is grouped in three trilogies: the Trilogy of Knowledge—*Eonul dogmatic* [*The Dogmatic Eon*], *Cunoaşterea luciferic* [*Luciferian Knowledge*], *Cenzura transcendentală* [*Transcendental Censorship*] (1943), the Trilogy of Culture—*Orizont şi stil* [*Horizon and Style*], *Spaţiul Mioritic* [*The Mioritic Space*], *Geneza metaforei şi sensul culturii* [*The Genesis of the Metaphor and Meaning of Culture*] (1944), and the Trilogy of Values—*Ştiinţă şi creaţie* [*Science and Creation*], *Gîndire magică şi religie* [*Magical Thought and Religion*], *Artă şi valoare* [*Art and Value*] (1946).

BOGZA, Geo (1908–1993). Romanian writer, poet, journalist, and theoretician of the avant-garde.

BRAGA, Corin (1961–). Romanian novelist and literary critic.

BRUMARU, Emil (1939–). Romanian poet and writer. Brumaru was a physician by profession, and practiced in Dolhasca, a small provincial town in Moldavia, from 1963 to 1975, before becoming a full-time writer. He joined the oneiric group in 1967. Tsepeneag describes Brumaru's Oneiricism as "domestic and at the same time perverse." The setting of many of Brumaru's lyrical poems is the kitchen, a zone of eroticized, sometimes even menacing foodstuffs and ineffable *Stimmung*. His volumes include *Versuri* [*Poems*] (Bucharest, Editura Albatros, 1970), *Detectivul Artur* [*Arthur the Detective*] (Bucharest, Editura Cartea Românească, 1970), *Julien Ospitalierul* [*Julian the Hospitaller*] (Bucharest, Editura Cartea

Românească, 1974), *Cîntece naive* [*Naïve Songs*] (Bucharest, Editura Cartea Românească, 1976), *Dulapul îndrăgostit* [*The Enamoured Cupboard*] (Bucharest, Editura Cartea Românească, 1980), *Ruina unui samovar* [*The Ruins of a Samovar*] (Bucharest, Editura Cartea Românească, 1983).

CARAGIALE, Ion Luca (1852–1912). Romanian writer and playwright. Caragiale was an incisive satirist of Romanian social and political mores. In 1904, he went into self-imposed exile in Berlin, disgusted by the scandal created by false accusations of plagiarism against him in the press, having uncovered the identity of the anonymous slanderer and won a libel case against him. Both in his lifetime and afterwards, Caragiale's work has earned high praise, but also furious opposition on the part of those indignant at his unsparing satirical portrayal of national flaws and weaknesses.

CESEREANU, Ruxandra (1963–). Romanian poet and novelist.

CHILATE. Tsepeneag would seem to be playing here on a phonetic peculiarity of the Moldavian dialect of Romanian, where the syllable "pi" in word initial position becomes "chi" (pronounced /ki:/), e.g. "chicior" for the standard "picior" (foot).

DIMOV, Leonid (1926–1987). Romanian poet, translator, essayist and, alongside Dumitru Tsepeneag, principal theorist of Oneiricism. Dimov stands out for his absolute and unwavering refusal to make any compromise, whether moral or aesthetic, with the Romanian communist regime.

During the Gheorghiu-Dej period, he was arrested for urinating against the plinth of a statue of Stalin, a gesture of symbolic defiance that might, in the context of the times, be interpreted as not merely reckless but even suicidal. Always living in precarious material circumstances, he did not make his literary debut until 1966, with a volume of poems entitled *Versuri* (Bucharest, Editura pentru Literatură). His other published volumes include: *Pe malul Stixului* [*On the Banks of the Styx*] (Bucharest, Editura Tineretului, 1968), *Carte de vise* [*Book of Dreams*] (Bucharest, Editura pentru Literatură, 1969), *Eleusis* (Bucharest, Cartea Românească, 1970), *A.B.C.* (Bucharest, Cartea Românească, 1973), *La Capăt* [*At the End*] (Bucharest, Editura Eminescu, 1974), *Spectacol* [*Performance*] (Bucharest, Cartea Românească, 1979), and *Veşnica întoarcere* [*Eternal Recurrence*] (Bucharest, Cartea Românească, 1982).

DOR (Latin *dolere*, to feel pain, ache, grieve), a Romanian multivalent word with meanings of *pain* (physical and/or psychical), *nostalgia, melancholy, sadness, pining, yearning* etc. In the philosophy of Lucian Blaga, the word *dor*, which is seen as untranslatable and irreducible, becomes a keyword expressive of the unique spiritual essence of the Romanian people.

GABREA, Florin (1943–). An architect by profession, Gabrea published a volume of oneiric prose entitled *Hanimore* (1968), which Dumitru Tsepeneag describes, in *Quelques idées fixes et autant de variables* (*Cahiers de l'Est*, no. 4,

1975), as follows: "Things here are viewed through the eyelashes but nevertheless described with the greatest exactitude: but only from close to, by isolating them. When the myopic eye draws back, you would think that water has filled the space between, making the outlines shimmer, shift, alter. For Florin Gabrea, the world is a vast aquarium."

GOMA, Paul (1935–). Romanian writer and dissident. First arrested and imprisoned (for two years) in 1956, while a student at Bucharest University, for organizing a students' movement in solidarity with the Hungarian Uprising. In 1977, he disseminated a letter in support of the Czechoslovakian Charter 77. He was arrested and tortured by the Securitate, but eventually allowed to go into exile in France, given international scrutiny of his case.

GROŞAN, Ioan (1954–). Romanian prose writer of the "Eighties Generation." His collection of novellas *Caravana cinematografică* [*The Cinema Caravan*] was published in 1985.

IVĂNCEANU, Vintilă (1940–2008). Romanian writer, poet and theater director. His works include a collection of oneiric poetry (*Cinste specială* [*Special Honor*], Bucharest, Editura pentru Literatură, 1967), the novels *Pînă la dispariţie* [*To the Point of Disappearance*] (Bucharest, Editura pentru Literatură, 1968) and *Nemaipomenitele păţanii ale lui Milorad de Bouteille* [*The Extraordinary Misadventures of Milorad de Bouteille*] (Bucharest, Editura Cartea Românească, 1970), and the burlesque oneiric epic poem

Vulcaloborgul şi frumoasa Beleponjă [*The Vulcaloborg and the Beautiful Beleponjă*] (Bucharest, Editura Cartea Românească, 1970). He left Romania in 1970 and settled in Austria, where he was part of the Viennese postmodern group and published numerous works in German.

IVĂNESCU, Mircea (1931–). Romanian poet, essayist and translator. Ivănescu is the Romanian translator of James Joyce (*Ulysses*), Franz Kafka, and Robert Musil.

LOVINESCU, Eugen (1881–1943). Romanian literary critic and prose writer. Author of the six-volume *Istoria literaturii române contemporane* [*The History of Contemporary Romanian Literature*] (1926–1929).

LUCA, Gherasim—pseudonym of Salman Locker (1913–1995). Jewish Romanian surrealist writer, poet, and artist. Persecuted in Romania, Luca managed to flee in 1952, and lived as a stateless refugee in Paris until his suicide in 1995.

MARIN, Mariana (1956–2003). Romanian poet of the "Eighties Generation."

MAZILESCU, Virgil (1942–1984). Romanian poet. Mazilescu worked variously as a country schoolteacher, librarian, and editorial assistant, leading a bohemian life at the margins of the communist society of the time. He published four volumes of poetry: *Versuri* [*Verses*] (Bucharest, Editura pentru Literatură, 1968), *Fragmente din regiunea de odinioară* [*Fragments from the Region of Yore*] (Bucharest, Editura Cartea Românească, 1970), *Va fi linişte, va fi seară* [*It will be quiet, it will be evening*] (Bucharest, Editura Cartea Românească, 1979), and *Guillaume poetul şi administratorul* [*Guillaume the Poet and the Superintendent*] (Bucharest, Editura Cartea Românească, 1983). His posthumously published diary, which covers the period from January 3 to April 25, 1984, shortly before his death, and which has been described as "the Apocalypse according to Virgil," is a harrowing account of his descent into despair and alcoholism (published in *Opere* [*Works*], ed. Alexandru Condeescu, Bucharest, Editura Muzeul Literaturii Române, 2003).

MIORITIC—adjective derived from the name of a folk ballad, *Mioriţa*, whose origins have been variously dated back to the sixteenth or early eighteenth century. In one of its versions, the ballad was first transcribed and published in 1850 by Vasile Alecsandri (1818–1890). The ballad tells the tale of three shepherds, one Moldavian, one Hungarian, and one Wallachian (in Alecsandri's version, the third shepherd is from the Vîlcea region, in order to avoid offending those who at the time were seeking the unification of the principalities of Wallachia and Moldavia, which came about in 1859). The Hungarian and the Wallachian plot to kill the Moldavian, who is "richer in flocks." A ewe lamb (*mioara*; *mioriţa* is the diminutive form) from the Moldavian's flock warns her master of the plot to kill him, in line with an ancient Balkan folk belief that sheep can foretell the nearness of death. The Moldavian shepherd fatalistically accepts his impending death, however, and expresses his desire to be buried according to the ancestral rites, whose ceremonials he metaphorically likens to a wedding. The funeral of the murdered shepherd is a cosmic wedding, at which the sun and the moon are the godparents, the firs and sycamores the wedding guests, the birds the musicians, and the bride, in some versions, a shooting star. The ewe lamb consoles the shepherd's grieving mother with an account of the wedding. Romanian philosopher Lucian Blaga (1895–1961), in *Spațiul Mioritic* [*The Mioritic Space*] (1936), sees the ballad as an expression of a fatalistic love of death in Romanian culture.

MOFTANGIU, pl. *moftangii*. The word, coined by Caragiale, is a comical formation from *moft* and the suffix *-giu* (from Turkish) to denote an occupation (e.g. *cafegiu*—coffee-shop keeper), trade (*halvagiu*—halva maker), or person prone to a particular vice or habit (e.g. *scandalagiu*—brawler). (Cf. Lazare Sainéan, "Les Éléments orientaux en roumain. 3. Considérations morphologiques," *Romania*, no. 3, Paris, 1902, 82–83.) Tiktin (1003) gives the definition "Flausen-, Phrasemacher, Blageur." In *Momente*, Caragiale includes three skits under the title "Moftangii": "Rromânul" [The Rromanian Man], "Rromâncă" [The Rromanian Woman] and "Savantul" [The Savant]. The double "rr" imitates the rolled "r" of the ludicrously fervent patriot when pronouncing his nationality.

MOFTOLOGICAL. The word m*oft*, plural *mofturi*, derives from a Turkish word meaning *free of charge, cheap*. In Romanian, the word has acquired the meaning *lacking in value, content or importance, a trifle, a lie, a swindle, empty words, palaver, humbug, poppycock* (see H. Tiktin, *Rumänische-*

deutsches Wörterbuch, vol. 2, Bucharest, Staatsdruckerei, 1915, 1003: "Wert-, Inhalts-, Bedeutungslosen, das den Anschein eines gewissen Wertes etc. hat: Mumpitz, Schwindel, Humbug, pl. Geflunker"). The word *moft* gains an emblematic status in Caragiale's sketches of social satire directed at "moftul român"—also the title of a satirical newspaper he published from 1893 to 1902: *Moftul român: Revista spiritistă națională, organ pentru răspîndirea științelor oculte în Dacia Traiană*" [*The Romanian Moft: National spiritist review, organ for dissemination of the occult sciences in Dacia Trajana*]. Caragiale defines *moft* in the following apostrophe: "O Moft! Thou art the watchword and motto of our times. Vast syllable of unbounded content, in thee there is such comfortable room for countless meanings: joys and misfortunes, merit and infamy, guilt and misadventure, right, duty, sentiments, interests, convictions, politics, plague, typhoid, diphtheria, destructive vices, suffering, poverty, talent and imbecility, lunar and mental eclipses, past, present, future—all of them, all these do we modern Romanians name in a single, short word: MOFT." The derivations *moftolog* (*moftologist*), *moftologic,* and *moftologie* (*moftology*) were coined by Caragiale (Tiktin, 1004).

MOMENTS. Caragiale published a collection of short satirical sketches entitled *Momente* [*Moments*], mostly directed at the *mofturi* of various social categories (Bucharest, 1901).

MUREȘAN, Ion (1955–). Romanian poet. Collections: *Cartea de iarnă* [*The Winter Book*], Bucharest, Cartea

Românească, 1981, *Poemul care nu poate fi înțeles* [*The Poem that cannot be Understood*], Tîrgu Mureş, Arhipelag, 1993. His poetry has been described as having "the power to transcend worn-out images and themes, to rise from the sphere of everyday banality into a space of visionariness often contiguous with the boundaries of pure poetry" (Nichita Danilov, *Apocalipsa de carton* [*Cardboard Apocalypse*], Jassy, Editura Institutul European, 1993, 40).

NAUM, Gellu (1915–2001). Romanian surrealist poet and novelist. In the first two decades of the communist regime, up until 1968, Naum was banned from publishing his work and made a precarious living through translations and literature for children. See *Vasco da Gama şi alte poheme/Vasco da Gama and Other Pohems*, ed., trans. and with an introduction by Alistair Ian Blyth, Bucharest, Editura Humanitas, 2007.

NEACŞU, Iulian (1941–). Romanian oneiric writer. He has published the following collections of short prose, *Iarna cînd e soare* [*Winter When it's Sunny*], Bucharest, Editura pentru Literatură, 1966; *Insul (Texte, semne, apocrife)* [*The Bloke (Texts, Signs, Apocrypha)*], Bucharest, Editura pentru Literatură, 1968; *Ora exactă* [*The Precise Time*], Bucharest: Editura Emninescu, 1996; *Un țăran trece strada* [*A Peasant Crosses the Street*], Bucharest, Editura Eminescu, 2001.

O SCRISOARE PIERDUTĂ (1884). A masterpiece of comic theater. The action takes place in a provincial town in the Carpathians, on the eve of a general election, which gives Caragiale plentiful material to expose and satirize political corruption; venality, hypocrisy and immorality in public office; tub-thumping jingoism; mawkish patriotic sentiment; favoritism and nepotism; demagogy; the vulgarity and unscrupulous ambition of the parvenu; and petty backstabbing. The lost letter of the title is a billet-doux which if made public would expose the adulterous love affair between Zoe, the wife of Zaharia Trahanache, president of all the town's various official committees, and Ştefan Tipătescu, the county prefect. The letter falls into the hands of demagogic, jingoist opposition candidate Nae Caţavencu (a lawyer and proprietor of *Răcnetul Carpaţilor* [*The Roar of the Carpathians*]), and much grotesque hilarity ensues.

PARASCHIVESCU, Miron Radu (1911–1971). Romanian poet and essayist.

PĂUN, Paul—pseudonym of Paul Zaharia (1915–1994). Romanian surrealist artist and writer. In 1931, he was prosecuted for obscenity, along with Gherasim Luca and other Romanian surrealists, for the publication of a magazine with the deliberately provocative and (still) shocking title *pula modernă* [*the modern cock*]. The trial was brought by eminent Romanian historian, *bourgeois épaté* and, at the time, Prime Minister Nicolae Iorga. Co author, with Gellu Naum and Virgil Teodorescu, of *Critica mizeriei* [*Critique of Misery, or: Poverty, or: Squalor*] (1945). Paul Păun died in exile in Haifa.

POL. In Romanian, "pol" means "pole," in the sense of "axis."

POP, Ioan Es. (1958–). Romanian poet, not published until after the 1989 Revolution.

POP, Sânziana (1939–). Romanian prose writer.

PROLETCULTISM. The official term for socialist realism in Romania. It derives from the Soviet portmanteau word "proletkult" (for *proletarskaja kul'tura*).

REBREANU, Liviu (1885–1944) was a major Romanian novelist of the first half of the twentieth century. *Ion, Blestemul pămîntului, blestemului iubirii* [*Ion, The Curse of the Earth, the Curse of Love*] (1920) is a social novel which recounts the tragedy of the eponymous hero, a landless peasant.

ROMANIAN VICTORY GRAND HOTEL. The Romanian victory referred to is that of 1877, in the Romanian War of Independence that freed the country from the Ottoman yoke. The novella, written from a first-person viewpoint, describes a nightmarish stay in the hotel of the title. The narrator arrives from Paris by train in a Bucharest that seems subtly altered, abandoned, sad, impoverished. Exhausted and indisposed, he decides to stay in the Romanian Victory Grand Hotel. The sinister, piercing glances of the other patrons in the bar and then the restaurant make him feel acutely ill at ease and so he decides to go to his room. However, he is unable to sleep because the bed is crawling with bugs, "an entire nation, as if at a plebiscite." He manages to snatch some sleep on the carpet on the floor, but is awoken by the hubbub of male and female revelers below his window, who spill from a café and a pub on the other side of the street ("Independence Street"), but are not allowed into the hotel to continue their debauch. The narrator witnesses a grotesque, primitive scene of drunken violence, during which a scantily clad, dissheveled woman is struck by a police sergeant and a dog is tortured to death.

SCHOOL OF RESENTMENT. The term was coined by Harold Bloom with reference to Marxist, feminist, African American etc. forms of critical interpretation, which attempt to undermine the Canon by demanding the inclusion of aesthetically inferior works on solely political grounds.

SIMIONESCU, Mircea Horia (1928–). Romanian prose writer. His first novel, *Dicționar onomastic* [*Onomastic Dictionary*] (1969), was the first in an experimental cycle (entitled *Ingeniosului bine temperat* [*The Well-Tempered Ingenioso*]) of ludic virtuosity, intended, as the author has jokingly observed, to compete with the telephone directory. The other volumes are: *Bibliografia generală* [*General Bibliography*] (1971), *Jumătate plus unu (Alt dicționar onomastic)* [*Half plus One (Another Onomastic Dictionary)*] (1976), *Breviarul (Historia calamitatum)* [*The Breviary (History of Calamities)*] (1980), and *Toxicologia sau Dincolo de bine și dincoace de rău* [*Toxicology, or Beyond Good and Hither of Evil*] (1983). Rejecting the literature of beginning-middle-end, Mircea Horia Simionescu writes books that he says are "good for reading however you like, on a park bench or up on a roof, in a tram or in an alpine cabin, starting from the middle, from back to front, from the bottom to the top of the page, like the almanacs and calendars of our ancestors, like notes and letters, like press releases."

STĂNESCU, Nichita (1933–1983). One of the most important and most original Romanian poets of the 1960s and '70s. Winner of the Herder Prize in 1975 and nominated for the Nobel Prize for Literature in 1980.

TĂNASE, Virgil (1945–). Romanian writer. Tănase studied Romance Languages at Bucharest University, graduating in 1968, and then film direction at the I. L. Caragiale Institute, graduating in 1975. He worked as a director at the National Theater in Jassy before settling in France in 1977. He published oneric short prose in literary magazines in Romania, but his oneiric novels *Portret de om cosind în peisaj marin* [*Portrait of a Man Reaping in a Seascape*] and *Apocalipsa unui adolescent de familie* [*Apocalypse of a Family Adolescent*], although accepted by Cartea Românească for publication, never went to press. They were later published in France, where the writer has enjoyed a prolific literary career in his adopted language.

TÎRGOVIŞTE SCHOOL. Group of postmodern Romanian prose writers who met in the Wallachian town of Tîrgovişte, including Radu Petrescu (1927–1982), Costache Olăreanu (1929–2000) and Mircea Horia Simionescu (1928–).

TEODORESCU, Virgil (1909–1987). Romanian poet who wrote in a surrealist manner before the communist period. In the 1950s he reinvented himself as a socialist-realist poet, and was rewarded with privileges and power, including the presidency of the Writers' Union and membership of the Romanian Academy. In the 1960s, he returned to an insipid form of surrealism, but still writing poems on officially approved communist subjects.

TEXTUALISM was a Romanian literary and theoretical movement of the 1980s, represented by novelists such as Gheorghe Crăciun (1950–2007) and Mircea Nedelciu (1950–1999) and literary critic and theorist Marin Mincu (1944–2009). The textualists, inspired by the theories propounded by *Tel Quel* in the 1960s, practiced a form of literature that set out to annihilate the author and any referent or object outside the text. The text was to be endlessly self-generating and self-mirroring, intersecting only with other texts. "Textualism" was thus a form of postmodernism that existed within a hard-line communist society.

TITEL, Sorin (1935–1985). Romanian novelist and prose writer. Titel studied film making at university but was expelled in 1956 for expressing solidarity with Hungarian students during the uprising that was subsequently crushed by the Soviets. He was readmitted as a part-time student in 1961 and graduated with a Degree in Philology in 1964. He published his first volume of short stories in 1963, entitled *Copacul* [*The Tree*] (Bucharest, Editura pentru Literatură). His novels *Dejunul pe iarbă* [*The Dinner on the Grass*] (Bucharest, Editura pentru Literatură, 1968) and *Lunga călătorie a prizonierului* [*The Long Journey of the Prisoner*]

(Bucharest, Editura Cartea Românească, 1971), and the collection of short stories *Noaptea inocenților* [*The Night of the Innocents*] (Bucharest, Editura Cartea Românească, 1970) are oneiric works, but afterwards Titel returned to a more realist style of writing.

TRANSFIGURATION OF ROMANIA. Published in Bucharest, in 1936. Cioran, mortified by his rash, hotheaded younger self, later repudiated the book, along with the fascist views held in his youth, and forbade translation or any further publication.

TRANSHUMANCE—ancient pastoral custom, in which the flocks are led up into or down from the mountains, which is still practiced in parts of Romania even today.

TROST, Dolfi (1916–1966). Romanian surrealist artist, poet, and inventor of "cubomania." The co-author, along with Gherasim Luca, of *Dialectique de la dialectique* (1945), and the *L'Infra-Noir* manifesto (1947), with Gellu Naum, Virgil Teodorescu, Gherasim Luca and Paul Păun. Trost died in exile in Chicago.

TURCEA, Daniel (1945–1979). Romanian poet. Turcea published two volumes of highly hermetic poetry, in which Oneiricism might be said to meet a cryptic form of hesychasm: *Entropia* (Bucharest, Cartea Românească, 1970) and *Epifania* (Bucharest, Cartea Românească, 1978). He was a convert to Orthodoxy and, suffering from leukemia, spent his final years in Cernica Monastery, near Bucharest, where he died at the age of just thirty-four. Given that he was a religious dissident active in the conversion to Orthodoxy of other writers and artists, the possibility that he was poisoned by the Securitate cannot be ruled out.

TZIGANIAD is a mock-heroic epic poem by Ion Budai-Deleanu (1760–1820), which describes the adventures of a band of gypsies conscripted by Vlad the Impaler to fight in the war against the invading Turks. The poem also features a Miltonic Satan and a descent to the underworld, described in grotesque terms of the lower corporeal stratum (e.g. sinners made into sausages by demon butchers to feed hungry little devils).

ULICI, Laurenţiu (1943–2000). Romanian literary critic.

URMUZ—pseudonym of Demetru Dem. Demetrescu-Buzău (1883–1923). Demetrescu-Buzău fought in the 1913 Balkan War and on his return to Romania worked as a clerk of court. In 1923, he shot himself, in what was an apparently premeditated gesture of senselessness, thus comparable to the suicide of Jacques Vaché (1919). Like Vaché, Urmuz was a surrealist *avant la lettre*. His *Pagini bizare* [*Bizarre Pages*], which circulated in manuscript among family and friends, anticipate both Surrealism and the literature of the absurd. Although his complete works consist of only nine short anti-prose pieces and one anti-poem, the posthumous influence of Urmuz was incalculable, both in Romania and, via Eugène Ionesco, beyond. Tudor Arghezi, who invented the name Urmuz, published the story "Pîlnia şi Stamate" [The Funnel and Stamate] in two consecutive issues of his magazine

Cugetul românesc in 1922, the only work by Demetrescu-Buzău to be published during his lifetime. For the Romanian avant-garde and surrealists, Urmuz would attain the status of an almost miraculous figure, their absolute precursor and model. The world created by Urmuz is one of advanced material deterioration, littered with worn-out junk (rusty funnels, old rags, a piano lid, perished rubber bladders, etc.), perhaps reminiscent of the underworld visited by Epistemon in Rabelais's *Pantagruel*. This world is peopled by strange zoomorphic and mechanomorphic creatures, such as Grummer, who has a beak made of aromatic wood, or Ismail, who "consists of eyes, sideburns and a frock" and walks a badger on a leash made from a ship's hawser.

UVEDENRODE. A poem by Ion Barbu first published in *Antologia poeților de azi* [*Anthology of the Poets of Today*], ed. Ion Pillat and Perpessicius, Bucharest, Cartea Românească, 1925. "In the chasm Uvedenrode / How many gastropods! / Suprasexual / Supramusical; // Gastropods! / Greatly limpid rhapsodes, / Modes of odes / Skies scarf / Antennae in harps: // Uvedenrode / Above modes and time / Olympus! // Hour in crystalline / Next to the virgin Geraldine! // Her lace / Like chainmail blossom, / Through her arms / Glaciers in ideas, / In the holy sun, / Equal—this hymn: // Ordered helix, / Sound / Fruit of lyre, / End pedagogic, / Cradle mythologic, // From the great tents / You appear: / O, billow horse / Above the mare / With the chalk overhead in a spiral! // Incarnate appetite, / See here a maid: / She glides once, / She glides twice / Or up to nine, / Until you swathe her / In slight tremors, / Until you spin her / Into gastropod chainmail; / Until, in slow / Attentive antennae / You lower her: // With pendulum slowness, / A useless package, / 'Neath time, / 'Neath modes, / Into Uvedenrode."

VIŞNIEC, Matei (1956–). Romanian poet, playwright and novelist. Vişniec fled Romania in 1987, gaining political asylum in France, where he is now a prolific creator of neo-absurdist theater.

LAURA PAVEL is a Romanian essayist and literary critic. She is Associate Professor at the Faculty of Theater and Television of the Babeş-Bolyai University, and Head of the Department of Theater Studies and Media.

ALISTAIR IAN BLYTH's translations from Romanian include the novel *Little Fingers* by Filip Florian and *An Intellectual History of Cannibalism* by Cătălin Avramescu.

SELECTED DALKEY ARCHIVE PAPERBACKS

Petros Abatzoglou, *What Does Mrs. Freeman Want?*
Michal Ajvaz, *The Golden Age.*
The Other City.
Pierre Albert-Birot, *Grabinoulor.*
Yuz Aleshkovsky, *Kangaroo.*
Felipe Alfau, *Chromos.*
Locos.
Ivan Ângelo, *The Celebration.*
The Tower of Glass.
David Antin, *Talking.*
António Lobo Antunes, *Knowledge of Hell.*
Alain Arias-Misson, *Theatre of Incest.*
Iftikhar Arif and Waqas Khwaja, eds., *Modern Poetry of Pakistan.*
John Ashbery and James Schuyler, *A Nest of Ninnies.*
Gabriela Avigur-Rotem, *Heatwave and Crazy Birds.*
Heimrad Bäcker, *transcript.*
Djuna Barnes, *Ladies Almanack.*
Ryder.
John Barth, *LETTERS.*
Sabbatical.
Donald Barthelme, *The King.*
Paradise.
Svetislav Basara, *Chinese Letter.*
René Belletto, *Dying.*
Mark Binelli, *Sacco and Vanzetti Must Die!*
Andrei Bitov, *Pushkin House.*
Andrej Blatnik, *You Do Understand.*
Louis Paul Boon, *Chapel Road.*
My Little War.
Summer in Termuren.
Roger Boylan, *Killoyle.*
Ignácio de Loyola Brandão, *Anonymous Celebrity.*
The Good-Bye Angel.
Teeth under the Sun.
Zero.
Bonnie Bremser, *Troia: Mexican Memoirs.*
Christine Brooke-Rose, *Amalgamemnon.*
Brigid Brophy, *In Transit.*
Meredith Brosnan, *Mr. Dynamite.*
Gerald L. Bruns, *Modern Poetry and the Idea of Language.*
Evgeny Bunimovich and J. Kates, eds., *Contemporary Russian Poetry: An Anthology.*
Gabrielle Burton, *Heartbreak Hotel.*
Michel Butor, *Degrees.*
Mobile.
Portrait of the Artist as a Young Ape.
G. Cabrera Infante, *Infante's Inferno.*
Three Trapped Tigers.
Julieta Campos, *The Fear of Losing Eurydice.*
Anne Carson, *Eros the Bittersweet.*
Orly Castel-Bloom, *Dolly City.*
Camilo José Cela, *Christ versus Arizona.*
The Family of Pascual Duarte.
The Hive.
Louis-Ferdinand Céline, *Castle to Castle.*
Conversations with Professor Y.
London Bridge.
Normance.
North.
Rigadoon.
Hugo Charteris, *The Tide Is Right.*
Jerome Charyn, *The Tar Baby.*
Eric Chevillard, *Demolishing Nisard.*
Marc Cholodenko, *Mordechai Schamz.*
Joshua Cohen, *Witz.*
Emily Holmes Coleman, *The Shutter of Snow.*
Robert Coover, *A Night at the Movies.*
Stanley Crawford, *Log of the S.S. The Mrs Unguentine.*
Some Instructions to My Wife.
Robert Creeley, *Collected Prose.*
René Crevel, *Putting My Foot in It.*
Ralph Cusack, *Cadenza.*
Susan Daitch, *L.C.*
Storytown.
Nicholas Delbanco, *The Count of Concord.*
Sherbrookes.
Nigel Dennis, *Cards of Identity.*
Peter Dimock, *A Short Rhetoric for Leaving the Family.*
Ariel Dorfman, *Konfidenz.*
Coleman Dowell, *The Houses of Children.*
Island People.
Too Much Flesh and Jabez.
Arkadii Dragomoshchenko, *Dust.*
Rikki Ducornet, *The Complete Butcher's Tales.*
The Fountains of Neptune.
The Jade Cabinet.
The One Marvelous Thing.
Phosphor in Dreamland.
The Stain.
The Word "Desire."
William Eastlake, *The Bamboo Bed.*
Castle Keep.
Lyric of the Circle Heart.
Jean Echenoz, *Chopin's Move.*
Stanley Elkin, *A Bad Man.*
Boswell: A Modern Comedy.
Criers and Kibitzers, Kibitzers and Criers.
The Dick Gibson Show.
The Franchiser.
George Mills.
The Living End.
The MacGuffin.
The Magic Kingdom.
Mrs. Ted Bliss.
The Rabbi of Lud.
Van Gogh's Room at Arles.
Annie Ernaux, *Cleaned Out.*
Lauren Fairbanks, *Muzzle Thyself.*
Sister Carrie.
Leslie A. Fiedler, *Love and Death in the American Novel.*
Juan Filloy, *Op Oloop.*
Gustave Flaubert, *Bouvard and Pécuchet.*
Kass Fleisher, *Talking out of School.*
Ford Madox Ford, *The March of Literature.*
Jon Fosse, *Aliss at the Fire.*
Melancholy.
Max Frisch, *I'm Not Stiller.*
Man in the Holocene.

FOR A FULL LIST OF PUBLICATIONS, VISIT:
www.dalkeyarchive.com

SELECTED DALKEY ARCHIVE PAPERBACKS

Carlos Fuentes, *Christopher Unborn.*
Distant Relations.
Terra Nostra.
Where the Air Is Clear.
Janice Galloway, *Foreign Parts.*
The Trick Is to Keep Breathing.
William H. Gass, *Cartesian Sonata and Other Novellas.*
Finding a Form.
A Temple of Texts.
The Tunnel.
Willie Masters' Lonesome Wife.
Gérard Gavarry, *Hoppla! 1 2 3.*
Making a Novel.
Etienne Gilson,
The Arts of the Beautiful.
Forms and Substances in the Arts.
C. S. Giscombe, *Giscome Road.*
Here.
Prairie Style.
Douglas Glover, *Bad News of the Heart.*
The Enamoured Knight.
Witold Gombrowicz,
A Kind of Testament.
Karen Elizabeth Gordon,
The Red Shoes.
Georgi Gospodinov, *Natural Novel.*
Juan Goytisolo, *Count Julian.*
Exiled from Almost Everywhere.
Juan the Landless.
Makbara.
Marks of Identity.
Patrick Grainville, *The Cave of Heaven.*
Henry Green, *Back.*
Blindness.
Concluding.
Doting.
Nothing.
Jiří Gruša, *The Questionnaire.*
Gabriel Gudding,
Rhode Island Notebook.
Mela Hartwig, *Am I a Redundant Human Being?*
John Hawkes, *The Passion Artist.*
Whistlejacket.
Aleksandar Hemon, ed.,
Best European Fiction.
Aidan Higgins, *A Bestiary.*
Balcony of Europe.
Bornholm Night-Ferry.
Darkling Plain: Texts for the Air.
Flotsam and Jetsam.
Langrishe, Go Down.
Scenes from a Receding Past.
Windy Arbours.
Keizo Hino, *Isle of Dreams.*
Kazushi Hosaka, *Plainsong.*
Aldous Huxley, *Antic Hay.*
Crome Yellow.
Point Counter Point.
Those Barren Leaves.
Time Must Have a Stop.
Naoyuki Ii, *The Shadow of a Blue Cat.*
Mikhail Iossel and Jeff Parker, eds.,
Amerika: Russian Writers View the United States.
Gert Jonke, *The Distant Sound.*
Geometric Regional Novel.
Homage to Czerny.
The System of Vienna.
Jacques Jouet, *Mountain R.*
Savage.
Upstaged.
Charles Juliet, *Conversations with Samuel Beckett and Bram van Velde.*
Mieko Kanai, *The Word Book.*
Yoram Kaniuk, *Life on Sandpaper.*
Hugh Kenner, *The Counterfeiters.*
Flaubert, Joyce and Beckett: The Stoic Comedians.
Joyce's Voices.
Danilo Kiš, *Garden, Ashes.*
A Tomb for Boris Davidovich.
Anita Konkka, *A Fool's Paradise.*
George Konrád, *The City Builder.*
Tadeusz Konwicki, *A Minor Apocalypse.*
The Polish Complex.
Menis Koumandareas, *Koula.*
Elaine Kraf, *The Princess of 72nd Street.*
Jim Krusoe, *Iceland.*
Ewa Kuryluk, *Century 21.*
Emilio Lascano Tegui, *On Elegance While Sleeping.*
Eric Laurrent, *Do Not Touch.*
Hervé Le Tellier, *The Sextine Chapel.*
A Thousand Pearls (for a Thousand Pennies)
Violette Leduc, *La Bâtarde.*
Edouard Levé, *Suicide.*
Suzanne Jill Levine, *The Subversive Scribe: Translating Latin American Fiction.*
Deborah Levy, *Billy and Girl.*
Pillow Talk in Europe and Other Places.
José Lezama Lima, *Paradiso.*
Rosa Liksom, *Dark Paradise.*
Osman Lins, *Avalovara.*
The Queen of the Prisons of Greece.
Alf Mac Lochlainn,
The Corpus in the Library.
Out of Focus.
Ron Loewinsohn, *Magnetic Field(s).*
Mina Loy, *Stories and Essays of Mina Loy.*
Brian Lynch, *The Winner of Sorrow.*
D. Keith Mano, *Take Five.*
Micheline Aharonian Marcom,
The Mirror in the Well.
Ben Marcus,
The Age of Wire and String.
Wallace Markfield,
Teitlebaum's Window.
To an Early Grave.
David Markson, *Reader's Block.*
Springer's Progress.
Wittgenstein's Mistress.
Carole Maso, *AVA.*
Ladislav Matejka and Krystyna Pomorska, eds.,
Readings in Russian Poetics: Formalist and Structuralist Views.
Harry Mathews,
The Case of the Persevering Maltese: Collected Essays.
Cigarettes.
The Conversions.
The Human Country: New and Collected Stories.
The Journalist.

FOR A FULL LIST OF PUBLICATIONS, VISIT:
www.dalkeyarchive.com

SELECTED DALKEY ARCHIVE PAPERBACKS

My Life in CIA.
Singular Pleasures.
The Sinking of the Odradek Stadium.
Tlooth.
20 Lines a Day.
JOSEPH MCELROY,
Night Soul and Other Stories.
THOMAS MCGONIGLE,
Going to Patchogue.
ROBERT L. MCLAUGHLIN, ED., *Innovations: An Anthology of Modern & Contemporary Fiction.*
ABDELWAHAB MEDDEB, *Talismano.*
HERMAN MELVILLE, *The Confidence-Man.*
AMANDA MICHALOPOULOU, *I'd Like.*
STEVEN MILLHAUSER,
The Barnum Museum.
In the Penny Arcade.
RALPH J. MILLS, JR.,
Essays on Poetry.
MOMUS, *The Book of Jokes.*
CHRISTINE MONTALBETTI, *Western.*
OLIVE MOORE, *Spleen.*
NICHOLAS MOSLEY, *Accident.*
Assassins.
Catastrophe Practice.
Children of Darkness and Light.
Experience and Religion.
God's Hazard.
The Hesperides Tree.
Hopeful Monsters.
Imago Bird.
Impossible Object.
Inventing God.
Judith.
Look at the Dark.
Natalie Natalia.
Paradoxes of Peace.
Serpent.
Time at War.
The Uses of Slime Mould: Essays of Four Decades.
WARREN MOTTE,
Fables of the Novel: French Fiction since 1990.
Fiction Now: The French Novel in the 21st Century.
Oulipo: A Primer of Potential Literature.
YVES NAVARRE, *Our Share of Time.*
Sweet Tooth.
DOROTHY NELSON, *In Night's City.*
Tar and Feathers.
ESHKOL NEVO, *Homesick.*
WILFRIDO D. NOLLEDO, *But for the Lovers.*
FLANN O'BRIEN,
At Swim-Two-Birds.
At War.
The Best of Myles.
The Dalkey Archive.
Further Cuttings.
The Hard Life.
The Poor Mouth.
The Third Policeman.
CLAUDE OLLIER, *The Mise-en-Scène.*
Wert and the Life Without End.
PATRIK OUŘEDNÍK, *Europeana.*
The Opportune Moment, 1855.
BORIS PAHOR, *Necropolis.*
FERNANDO DEL PASO,
News from the Empire.
Palinuro of Mexico.
ROBERT PINGET, *The Inquisitory.*
Mahu or The Material.
Trio.
MANUEL PUIG,
Betrayed by Rita Hayworth.
The Buenos Aires Affair.
Heartbreak Tango.
RAYMOND QUENEAU, *The Last Days.*
Odile.
Pierrot Mon Ami.
Saint Glinglin.
ANN QUIN, *Berg.*
Passages.
Three.
Tripticks.
ISHMAEL REED,
The Free-Lance Pallbearers.
The Last Days of Louisiana Red.
Ishmael Reed: The Plays.
Juice!
Reckless Eyeballing.
The Terrible Threes.
The Terrible Twos.
Yellow Back Radio Broke-Down.
JOÃO UBALDO RIBEIRO, *House of the Fortunate Buddhas.*
JEAN RICARDOU, *Place Names.*
RAINER MARIA RILKE, *The Notebooks of Malte Laurids Brigge.*
JULIÁN RÍOS, *The House of Ulysses.*
Larva: A Midsummer Night's Babel.
Poundemonium.
Procession of Shadows.
AUGUSTO ROA BASTOS, *I the Supreme.*
DANIËL ROBBERECHTS,
Arriving in Avignon.
JEAN ROLIN, *The Explosion of the Radiator Hose.*
OLIVIER ROLIN, *Hotel Crystal.*
ALIX CLEO ROUBAUD, *Alix's Journal.*
JACQUES ROUBAUD, *The Form of a City Changes Faster, Alas, Than the Human Heart.*
The Great Fire of London.
Hortense in Exile.
Hortense Is Abducted.
The Loop.
The Plurality of Worlds of Lewis.
The Princess Hoppy.
Some Thing Black.
LEON S. ROUDIEZ, *French Fiction Revisited.*
RAYMOND ROUSSEL, *Impressions of Africa.*
VEDRANA RUDAN, *Night.*
STIG SÆTERBAKKEN, *Siamese.*
LYDIE SALVAYRE, *The Company of Ghosts.*
Everyday Life.
The Lecture.
Portrait of the Writer as a Domesticated Animal.
The Power of Flies.
LUIS RAFAEL SÁNCHEZ,
Macho Camacho's Beat.
SEVERO SARDUY, *Cobra & Maitreya.*
NATHALIE SARRAUTE,
Do You Hear Them?
Martereau.
The Planetarium.

FOR A FULL LIST OF PUBLICATIONS, VISIT:
www.dalkeyarchive.com

SELECTED DALKEY ARCHIVE PAPERBACKS

ARNO SCHMIDT, *Collected Novellas.*
Collected Stories.
Nobodaddy's Children.
Two Novels.
ASAF SCHURR, *Motti.*
CHRISTINE SCHUTT, *Nightwork.*
GAIL SCOTT, *My Paris.*
DAMION SEARLS, *What We Were Doing and Where We Were Going.*
JUNE AKERS SEESE,
Is This What Other Women Feel Too?
What Waiting Really Means.
BERNARD SHARE, *Inish.*
Transit.
AURELIE SHEEHAN,
Jack Kerouac Is Pregnant.
VIKTOR SHKLOVSKY, *Bowstring.*
Knight's Move.
A Sentimental Journey: Memoirs 1917–1922.
Energy of Delusion: A Book on Plot.
Literature and Cinematography.
Theory of Prose.
Third Factory.
Zoo, or Letters Not about Love.
CLAUDE SIMON, *The Invitation.*
PIERRE SINIAC, *The Collaborators.*
JOSEF ŠKVORECKÝ, *The Engineer of Human Souls.*
GILBERT SORRENTINO,
Aberration of Starlight.
Blue Pastoral.
Crystal Vision.
Imaginative Qualities of Actual Things.
Mulligan Stew.
Pack of Lies.
Red the Fiend.
The Sky Changes.
Something Said.
Splendide-Hôtel.
Steelwork.
Under the Shadow.
W. M. SPACKMAN,
The Complete Fiction.
ANDRZEJ STASIUK, *Fado.*
GERTRUDE STEIN,
Lucy Church Amiably.
The Making of Americans.
A Novel of Thank You.
LARS SVENDSEN, *A Philosophy of Evil.*
PIOTR SZEWC, *Annihilation.*
GONÇALO M. TAVARES, *Jerusalem.*
Learning to Pray in the Age of Technology.
LUCIAN DAN TEODOROVICI,
Our Circus Presents . . .
STEFAN THEMERSON, *Hobson's Island.*
The Mystery of the Sardine.
Tom Harris.
JOHN TOOMEY, *Sleepwalker.*
JEAN-PHILIPPE TOUSSAINT,
The Bathroom.
Camera.
Monsieur.
Running Away.
Self-Portrait Abroad.
Television.
DUMITRU TSEPENEAG,
Hotel Europa.
The Necessary Marriage.
Pigeon Post.
Vain Art of the Fugue.
ESTHER TUSQUETS, *Stranded.*
DUBRAVKA UGRESIC,
Lend Me Your Character.
Thank You for Not Reading.
MATI UNT, *Brecht at Night.*
Diary of a Blood Donor.
Things in the Night.
ÁLVARO URIBE AND OLIVIA SEARS, EDS.,
Best of Contemporary Mexican Fiction.
ELOY URROZ, *Friction.*
The Obstacles.
LUISA VALENZUELA, *Dark Desires and the Others.*
He Who Searches.
MARJA-LIISA VARTIO,
The Parson's Widow.
PAUL VERHAEGHEN, *Omega Minor.*
BORIS VIAN, *Heartsnatcher.*
LLORENÇ VILLALONGA, *The Dolls' Room.*
ORNELA VORPSI, *The Country Where No One Ever Dies.*
AUSTRYN WAINHOUSE, *Hedyphagetica.*
PAUL WEST,
Words for a Deaf Daughter & Gala.
CURTIS WHITE,
America's Magic Mountain.
The Idea of Home.
Memories of My Father Watching TV.
Monstrous Possibility: An Invitation to Literary Politics.
Requiem.
DIANE WILLIAMS, *Excitability: Selected Stories.*
Romancer Erector.
DOUGLAS WOOLF, *Wall to Wall.*
Ya! & John-Juan.
JAY WRIGHT, *Polynomials and Pollen.*
The Presentable Art of Reading Absence.
PHILIP WYLIE, *Generation of Vipers.*
MARGUERITE YOUNG, *Angel in the Forest.*
Miss MacIntosh, My Darling.
REYOUNG, *Unbabbling.*
VLADO ŽABOT, *The Succubus.*
ZORAN ŽIVKOVIĆ, *Hidden Camera.*
LOUIS ZUKOFSKY, *Collected Fiction.*
SCOTT ZWIREN, *God Head.*